INTERNATIONAL RESEARCH FORUM 2006

INTERNATIONAL RESEARCH FORUM 2006

LUTZ HEUSER, CLAUDIA ALSDORF, AND DAN WOODS

Evolved
Technologist
Press
New York, NY

International Research Forum 2006
Lutz Heuser, Claudia Alsdorf, and Dan Woods

Published by Evolved Technologist Press, an imprint of Evolved Media Network, 242 West 30th Street, Suite 801, New York, New York 10001

This book may be purchased for educational, business, or sales promotional use. For more information contact:

Evolved Technologist Press
(646) 827-2196
info@EvolvedTechnologist.com
www.EvolvedTechnologist.com

Editors: Dan Woods, Deb Cameron
Writers: John Verity, Dan Woods, Greg Lindsay, John Biggs
Copyeditor: Deb Cameron
Production Editor: Deb Gabriel
Proofreader: David Penick
Cover and Interior Design: 1106 Design
Illustrator: Tory Moore
First Edition: April 2007

ISBN: 978-0-9789218-1-1; 0-9789218-1-X

Contents

Preface

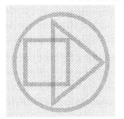

One of the sublime rewards of a career in research is that thinking and acting on innovative ideas is a part of your daily work. Normally, only in graduate school or in the planning stages of a new enterprise does one get to look at the big picture, find opportunities, and brainstorm about how to fill them. At SAP Research, we are fortunate. We not only are asked to analyze emerging trends and propose new ideas, but we then get to help put them to work inside our products.

In 2006, SAP Research helped fulfill its mission by bringing together 27 technology intellectuals for a day-long conference in Darmstadt, Germany to discuss four trends that were reshaping the technology business and the forces driving them. The attendees of the **International Research Forum 2006** spent an exciting day analyzing the meaning, structure, and impact of Web 2.0, Information Technology (IT) Security, Real World Awareness, and IT as a Tool for Growth and Development.

What we found is that bringing together so many smart people for such a conference is a much better way to raise questions than to answer them. At the end of each session, the contents of which we have captured in this book, we all felt excited but a bit disappointed that there was no time to dig deeper and to explore in greater detail the ideas that had emerged.

It then occurred to us that the work of the conference need not stop. We analyzed the transcripts of the proceedings and set to work on organizing the ideas and then invited others to become virtual participants to help move the discussion forward and provide additional analysis of the questions raised outside the strict time constraints of the forum itself.

We were fortunate that the response to our request for virtual participation was enthusiastic. Thought leaders such as Tim O'Reilly of O'Reilly Media, Tim Wood of the Grameen Foundation, Lee Felsenstein of the Fonly Institute, and noted security expert Bill Cheswick spent valuable time reviewing the ideas in their areas of expertise and added a new level of analysis and insight that organized and completed, in an important way, the discussions at the forum. Participants at the forum, such as Michael Schrage of the MIT Media Lab, Claudia Funke of McKinsey, Elgar Fleisch of the University of St. Gallen, in Switzerland, and Pradeep Khosla of Carnegie-Mellon University, also weighed in after the forum in separate interviews and added their thoughts.

While many books could be written about each of the topics covered, virtually no other book contains such a wide survey of ideas about technology from so many thinkers with such deep experience. Now that we are done, we are thrilled that this book not only captures the excitement of attending the conference but also leads the reader somewhere, sometimes to a new insight, sometimes to a new way of working, but always to ideas that can not just be thought about but applied.

We are so pleased with the result you are holding in your hands that we are changing the way we run the International Research Forum 2007 to make it even more effective and to facilitate collecting ideas for further analysis in a subsequent title.

Our sincere hope is that you find these ideas and this book exciting and that they help you in your work. We would love to hear about your experience with this book. Please visit us on the Internet at *http://www.international-research-forum.com* and share your thoughts.

Lutz Heuser

Acknowledgments

Every book is a team effort, but a book like this one is even more so. The authors' first debt goes to the participants at the 2006 International Research Forum and the virtual participants who joined us afterward. They are the core of this book and we are grateful for their time and enthusiasm. Please see the appendix for a full list of all those who are due our deepest thanks. We would also like to thank Tony Bradley, author of *Essential Computer Security* and moderator of the security area on About.com, whom we interviewed at the very end of our writing cycle. Although we cannot include you in our virtual participants, your contribution is nonetheless important. Special thanks also go to Prof. Encarnação of the Technical University of Darmstadt who was our host at the Fraunhofer Institute in Darmstadt for the conference.

The team at SAP Research captured the conference expertly through recordings, transcripts, and mind maps, that provided an excellent start for the writing team. We would like to especially thank Tanja Uermoesi for her hard work in helping us gather all the materials to prepare this book and coordinate the many interviews we conducted. Claudia Heimann, who served as moderator of the forum, played an important role in keeping the discussion flowing and orderly, which helped us tremendously in the preparation of this book. We would also like to thank Henrike Paetz and her team at SAP Research Communications for the enormous effort in organizing the event.

The writing team of John Verity, John Biggs, and Greg Lindsay transformed raw transcripts and interviews into a pleasing narrative. The editorial team at Evolved Media Network was a pleasure to work with. Deb Cameron and Deb Gabriel were expert editors who squeezed every error out of the text and attacked the job of getting the manuscript approved and into its final form with extreme diligence. Deb Gabriel's work as production editor kept us on schedule. David Penick gave the entire manuscript a careful proofreading. Tory Moore's illustrations and the cover and interior design work from Michele DeFilippo and her team at 1106 Design make the book attractive and easy on the eyes.

No expression of gratitude would be complete without adding our thanks to Peter Zencke, the responsible board member for SAP Research at SAP AG, Henning Kagermann, the CEO of SAP, and the rest of the executive board for their vision and support of this project.

Introduction

On March 27, 2006, more than two dozen academics, technologists, policymakers, entrepreneurs, and assorted intellectuals settled into a sunny, cozy room at the Fraunhofer Institute for Computer Graphics in Darmstadt, Germany. The day's agenda was straightforward: question, discuss, debate, and frame the future of information and communication technologies (ICT). There were no slides, no speeches, and no shilling for one's own projects. There were no deals to be struck in the hallways and no photographers to pose for. But there was just enough time for challenging a few handfuls of the world's brightest minds to propose solutions to a few of the gravest technological challenges of the 21st century (with the occasional break for *kaffee und kuchen*).

By that evening, as the First International Research Forum was winding down over dinner, everyone present was aware that they had participated in a remarkable event. There, under the auspices of SAP Research, these thinkers had zeroed in on and explored some of the most vexing issues in ICT: the evolution of the Web to Web 2.0 and beyond, the unprecedented deluge of data from real world awareness (RWA) technologies, the challenge of security in increasingly distributed systems, and how nations might harness ICT in the next wave of global growth.

They left Darmstadt the next morning with no grand plans or immediate solutions; they knew going in that the scope of the challenge was too great to produce any but the most vexing questions and embryonic answers. But the organizers had intended all along for the

Technology has the power to change the world, and thought has the power to change technology.

forum to be the foundation for a greater open-ended conversation that continues today in technology and policy circles, and now in the pages of this book.

International Research Forum 2006 is an attempt to capture this thought-provoking conference between two covers. In order to give the conference life beyond these pages, the authors invited a collection of virtual participants to expand on the issues raised at the forum. This chorus of luminaries (see "Virtual Participants" in the Appendix) expanded the lines of thinking with their unique critiques, proposals, and personal stratagems. The authors interviewed each of these virtual participants based on forum discussions, and their contributions are captured in the second half of each of the chapters.

The authors of this book, Prof. Lutz Heuser, Claudia Alsdorf, and Dan Woods, each played a critical role in organizing the forum's roster of speakers, guiding the day's sweeping discussions, and recruiting the auxiliary corps of thinkers who have carried its themes forward. In this book, they analyze the four megatrends assigned for that spring day in Darmstadt: Web 2.0 and the Semantic Web, IT Security, RWA, and IT as a Tool for Growth and Development. Each receives its own chapter here, even though the debates contained under each heading ranged further afield than their narrow labels might suggest (a map in each of these chapters serves to orient the reader visually to the breadth of the

---

Virtual Participants

Bill Cheswick, security expert, author, and consultant

Lee Felsenstein, cofounder of the Fonly Institute

Mark Kobayashi-Hillary, Director of the UK National Outsourcing Association

John Musser, Editor, ProgrammableWeb.com

Nandan Nilekani, CEO, Infosys Technologies

Tim O'Reilly, CEO, O'Reilly Media

Tim Wood, Technical Project Manager at the Grameen Technology Center

Greg Wyler, CEO, Terracom

---

discussion). As the day wore on, deeper themes crisscrossing the stated topics slowly emerged—ideas such as the hub-and-edge model of ICT, Enterprise 2.0, and hidden inequities buried in the overly simplistic idea of the flat world.

Although these themes are not isolated and explored within the body of the book, they will be discussed in passing here, after an overview of the megatrends, to provide context and enhance the reader's appreciation of their underlying significance.

Megatrend 1: Web 2.0 and the Semantic Web

Although the participants could have spent the entire session arguing over an exact definition of Web 2.0, it proved to be a fertile topic, setting the stage for many of the day's (and this book's) discussions. The core principle of Web 2.0, argues Tim O'Reilly, is the idea of "the Web as platform." The test of any true Web 2.0 service or application in this formulation, he insists, is an inherent degree of openness.

The stars of Web 2.0, such as Google, Amazon, and social networking sites like MySpace and Flickr, have all prospered by being "consumer-facing"—by appealing directly to their users for features and content. Google Maps' open application program interfaces (APIs), for example, popularized the concept of mashups—applications that combine data and functionality openly borrowed from different sources. Amazon has begun offering customers access to its own computing platform, data storage, and high-reliability hosting, and social networks like Flickr gain strength as millions of users aggregate personal contributions into giant taxonomies of valuable, searchable data.

Each of these applications embodies many of the other principles that are inextricably linked to Web 2.0: lightweight design and rapid assembly, a reliance on user-supplied data, many-to-many connections, and emergent features and behaviors that are apparent only after the platform and its audience have achieved sufficient scale. Web 2.0 applications are natural beneficiaries of network effects, increasing almost exponentially in value as the size of the network increases and then distributing that value across the network itself.

As profound as the shift from Web 1.0 to Web 2.0 has been, however, the potentially impending evolution to the Semantic Web sparked the most debate at the forum. Brainchild of World Wide Web inventor Tim Berners-Lee, the Semantic Web is one in which all the information on the Web is understandable and consumable by machines as well as humans. Abundant in metadata, the Semantic Web would empower applications to discover, understand, and utilize even unfamiliar data or services, holding out the possibility that the third iteration of the Web might flower with even more unforeseen connections and recombinations, producing still-greater benefits and potential new uses.

Megatrend 2: IT Security

Even as Web 2.0 and the Semantic Web promise ever-greater degrees of openness between systems, the list of threats that exploit and compromise that openness continues to mount. Hackers, malicious "script kiddies," identity thieves, criminal organizations, and even terrorists headline the rogues gallery imperiling the Web. Protecting data against unauthorized copying and viewing; blocking viruses, worms, and denial-of-service attacks; thwarting attempts to hijack enterprise applications; and managing individuals' access to networks and applications has become a $200 billion industry, one that forum participant Claudia Funke, Director in the Munich office of McKinsey & Company, described as "a big gold mine."

At the moment, that gold mine more closely resembles a large hole in the ground. Despite the sums being spent, holes and weaknesses still abound. A perfectly secure, perfectly open system is impossible to build; even with Microsoft's long and expensive campaign to build a perfectly secure browser, Internet Explorer 7 was hopelessly compromised within hours of its release. So how does one balance the demands of total security and total transparency on the one hand with fluid sharing of information and privacy concerns on the other?

The debate over that balance is waged at every level of the enterprise: which systems prize openness over stricter security, and which ones must be secure at all costs? Can any system exposed to the Internet ever be made secure considering how many of the Net's own components are less than fully accounted for? The same tradeoffs come into play with costs—where and how should organizations triage their resources? And what framework should one use for even making those judgments?

New technologies, such as biometric scanning with its promise of watertight user authentication, create extremely knotty legal and policy concerns. What are the privacy rights in such a system? And what are the individual user's responsibilities inside such a totalizing framework? That discussion opened the door at the forum to debates over whether it is feasible to legislate better software design, and if so, whether software should be more actively policed by law enforcement agencies. If not, could the threat of financial liability be enough to motivate companies to create more secure systems? And if either branch of "the stick" fails, then perhaps the "carrot" might still succeed—as Ms. Funke noted during the forum, security investments in the financial services industry have been found to improve profit margins by as much as 0.5 percent. That may be all the motivation the private sector needs to come up with solutions.

Megatrend 3: Real World Awareness

In tandem with the notion of the Semantic Web, real world awareness (RWA) is perceived as another key emerging theme in ICT's continuing evolution. The essence of RWA is the automated collection of real-time data from the physical world via an array of intelligent, connected sensors, and then parsing the data into information and filtering it in useful and beneficial ways.

The most common example of RWA is the use of radio-frequency ID (RFID) tags to track the movement of goods and materials through supply chains. Wal-Mart, for example, has mandated that its suppliers begin RFID-tagging their shipments at the pallet level, which would theoretically afford the retailing giant the ability to monitor its entire supply chain electronically, with little human intervention. Other potential uses of RWA include the application of sensors to detect temperature or pressure in factories and cars, vibrations in jet engines during flight, and remote monitoring and controlling of energy usage in homes. Still another use is the combination of wireless networks and GPS (global positioning system) signals to track the location of mobile computing devices—cellular phones, laptops, cars, and so on.

The great promise of RWA, forum participants agreed, is automation—systems will be able to collect data without human intervention or errors and use it to react to events more quickly and effectively. In other words, the faster the system "learns" what is happening, the faster it is able to analyze data and route information to the appropriate human agent, a model commonly referred to as "management by exception."

The potential pitfalls of RWA, the participants also agreed, lie in execution. As the cost of RFID tags and sensors falls, due to Moore's Law and economies of scale, tagging promises (or threatens?) to become pervasive. This has already sparked a backlash from some consumer rights groups, which are less afraid of police-state surveillance than they are of corporations assembling a 360-degree view of their consumption patterns from various databases and using that information to pitch them incessantly.

Forum participants had more prosaic concerns: How do you build systems that aren't overwhelmed by the "floods" and "torrents" of data certain to be generated from millions of sensors continually producing data? Perhaps initial mining and analysis should be performed at the edges of RWA networks, where noise can be filtered out and meaningful information passed along to enterprise applications. But security and privacy concerns may stymie such efforts. And then there is the question of standards—as of right now, there aren't many. Before RWA technologies become widespread, formatting, filtering, and routing protocols need to be built.

Megatrend 4: IT as a Tool for Growth and Development

The Euro-centric nature of the forum became clear only when the discussion shifted to the issues surrounding the use of ICT as a tool for national growth. For example, rather than invite a speaker who embodies the innovation (and swagger) of Silicon Valley, the forum asked Fabio Colasanti, the architect of the European Union's star-crossed "Lisbon strategy," to open the topic.

Conceived in March 2000, the Lisbon strategy was the E.U.'s 10-year plan to "make Europe, the most competitive and the most dynamic knowledge-based economy in the world," according to its stated objective. Instigated by the relative stagnation of the E.U. at a time when the rest of the world was growing rapidly, the Lisbon strategy was seen as a way to use technology as a lever to push through the structural reforms that many member nations desperately needed. What he and the E.U. learned, Mr. Colasanti ruefully admitted, was that while ICT possessed the power to accelerate economic growth and dynamism, it didn't have the power to institute change on its own.

His remarks set the tone for a soul-searching session in which participants debated Europe's slipping position in the global economy for ICT services. While U.S. companies have once again led the way with Web 2.0 technologies, the leaders of the developing world—China, India, and other Asian nations—threaten to commoditize the bottom of the ICT value chain. Ms. Funke warned the audience that "it is five minutes to midnight" on the metaphorical Doomsday Clock, while others argued that European firms needed to focus on better uses of ICT rather than attempt to build up Europe's ICT sector. They cited European automakers as one of the best examples of a native industry that not only uses embedded ICT to define its products but also to refine its processes. Still others argued that Europe had the chance to lead the way in systems integration, carving out a niche between the U.S. and offshoring nations.

The focus on Europe consumed much of the session, leaving it to the auxiliary corps of thinkers invited to contribute to this book—such as Infosys Technologies CEO Nandan Nilekani and technologists such as Greg Wyler and Lee Felsenstein—to continue the discussion here. Is it enough for nations in the developing world to merely *consume* ICT, using lightweight devices such as mobile phones or educational efforts like the "$100 Laptop" to connect to the Web, or is it essential that they produce ICT services as well? Even more critical is the question of whether developing nations can leapfrog the historical industrial phase of economic development straight to a post-industrial one based on ICT. The answer to this last question could prove to have enormous ramifications for education, energy, and the environment, to say the least.

The Hub-and-Edge Model of IT

Perhaps the greatest underlying concern of the forum, at least at a technical level, is the looming evolutionary shift in the structure and architecture of IT. The classical model of enterprise architecture places enterprise applications at the core of the business, where they are expected to automate and authenticate stable business processes and master data. The disadvantage of this model, of course, is that it is essentially static—it has led to applications that are so difficult to change and reconfigure that it is all but impossible to adapt them to evolving business processes. One could describe this as a purely "hub" architecture of IT—applications rest at the center of the organization, powerful but inaccessible to all but the most expert user.

The philosophy of Web 2.0 sits in fundamental opposition to this model, however. The opening of APIs and the creation of web services has created a mindset and an architecture in which the functionality contained within applications has been broken down into its constituent parts (services) and recombined in new ways (mashups). One can see in the tenets of Web 2.0—which include openness, decentralization, a relentless focus on the user and interface, and the notion of a perpetual beta—a potential paradox as far as most corporate IT environments are concerned. While Web 2.0's strengths complement the weaknesses of classical enterprise architectures, it is nearly impossible to actually realize these strengths if they are subjected to the same policies and policing as enterprise applications.

It is slowly becoming clear, then, that what's needed is a hub-and-edge model of IT, in which core systems continue their tasks while users on the edges of the organization create new services and applications that serve their immediate and changing personal needs. (As it turns out, perhaps you can have it both ways.)

The hub-and-edge model appeared again and again in the subtext of the four megatrends discussed during the forum. The Web 2.0 session served as a means for introducing the topic, along with the idea of Enterprise 2.0 (discussed in more detail later in this chapter).

RWA technologies are nothing but edge—billions and billions of tiny data-generating entities hovering at the literal edge of networks. At one point, the debate shifted to the question of whether existing enterprise resource planning (ERP) systems are adequately prepared for the torrents of data about to stream their way, or whether some sort of preliminary processing would be necessary. The impending need to embed some measure of analytical intelligence at the edge of the network in order to filter data flowing to core systems is a near-perfect example of edge computing evolution, and it is because of this shift, Dr. Pradeep Khosla suggested in the security session, that network security will have to undergo a fundamental transformation as well.

"Sensor networks are reaching into every nook and cranny of an organization's facilities," Dr. Khosla said. "As a result of this great expansion on the network, security is going to change from purely computer-based and OS-based to large-scale, IT-infrastructure-based." But how do you marry the mission-critical security needs of hub systems with the openness of Web 2.0 applications? One answer is: you don't. Instead, federated security models may end up partitioning organizations' systems into outward-facing edges, while hub systems are locked behind walls of drastically tighter security. A one-size-fits-all approach is increasingly untenable.

The theme even appeared in discussions of India and the developing world, although in that context it was a question of whether these nations could get by on IT infrastructures that are pure "edge." This was the subtext of notions such as "constraint-based development" in areas where the massive investment needed to install hub systems was infeasible (not to mention overkill). Michael Schrage, a researcher at the Massachusetts Institute of Technology (MIT) Media Lab, wondered aloud whether scripting languages and other lightweight programming techniques might be enough to produce services that deliver the proverbial 80 percent of the value at 20 percent (or less) of the developed world's costs. Efforts such as Nicholas Negroponte's "One Laptop Per Child" initiative, or Intel's competing vision with its "World Ahead" program, are essentially designed to create an edge of new users who are connecting to the Net via laptops and ultralightweight devices such as mobile phones. The edge, essentially, is everywhere.

Enterprise 2.0

It would be a mistake to assume that the hub-and-edge model is really a case of hub versus edge, with the two models competing to become the architecture of the future. But it's not hard to see why one might draw that conclusion, especially when users are flocking in droves to simple, lightweight tools that do the same jobs as industrial-strength applications, only with much less fuss. This is already the case with publishing and collaboration tools such as blogs, wikis, instant messaging, and even online calendar and scheduling systems. In many of these cases, users even take great pains to hide their usage of these tools, fearing that they'll be forced to give them up by the powers-that-be. (This phenomenon even has a name: "shadow IT.")

But the conceptual underpinnings of Web 2.0 are also transforming the architectures of enterprise applications as well. The opening of APIs by the likes of Google, Amazon, and eBay heralded the rise of web services, which in turn pointed the way toward service-oriented architectures (SOA). SOA paves the way for the transformation of applications into discrete services, and of bundled applications into software-as-a-service. The implications of this shift are tremendous, because they raise the possibility that rank-and-file employees may finally be offered the chance to both restructure IT so that it supports their business processes (rather than the other way around, as it has traditionally been done), and create their own services as needed, thus unleashing latent innovation within the organization.

The "Flat World" and the Tilted One

At the core of the larger discussion about IT and growth is a larger debate about the so-called "flat world," a reference to Thomas L. Friedman's hugely influential 2005 book, *The World Is Flat*. Friedman begins from the premise that advances in bandwidth and enterprise computing have made it possible for any ICT firm to compete globally. This idea, as simple (and simplistic) as it sounds, has tremendous implications for projections of economic growth in the 21st century. If, like Friedman, one believes that the metaphorical "pie" is growing—and thus we might all have a piece of it—then the flat world is nothing but opportunity. If one takes a more Malthusian view, however, then the flat world threatens to commoditize, outsource, and offshore a steadily increasing proportion of the ICT value chain.

These competing world views can be heard echoing throughout the discussion of ICT as a tool for growth; the participants aren't sure whether Europe should be helping the nations of the developing world, or competing with them. And while techno-optimists such as MIT's Nicholas Negroponte extol the virtues of the $100 Laptop and similar initiatives, there is an equally large camp of technologists who believe that these efforts essentially amount to digital colonialism. Are the peoples of the developing world a new market to be exploited or our peers who need a hand to lift them up? Alas, this was still another question that was left unresolved.

It is clear from this introduction that the forum covered a massive amount of intellectual territory in just one day. While the authors found no common thread in all of the ideas that swirled around the forum, which were then captured and analyzed for this book, there was a common feeling: the joy of learning and discovery. We know this book will introduce some new thinkers to you. Our hope in presenting this material to you is that you discover some ideas and perspectives that help you to put technology to work in your life in a better way.

Web 2.0 and the Semantic Web

It started as a curiosity, a catch-phrase adopted by venture capital-ists, entrepreneurs, and the press as shorthand for a renewed surge of Web-based startup companies. Among the first of these so-called Web 2.0 companies were several offering blogging tools and wikis, fol-lowed by social networking web sites aimed mainly at young people. They had a different feel than first-generation Web companies, a new modus operandi and philosophy that emphasized users and user-generated content. The idea morphed and flourished. And now, close to three years later, Web 2.0 refers to a collection of powerful new ideas and techniques that are reshaping IT and changing how enterprises as well as individuals will work with, create, and profit from information technology.

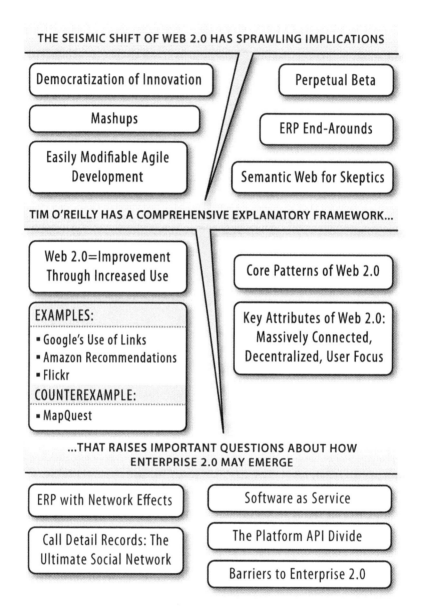

THE SEISMIC SHIFT OF WEB 2.0 HAS SPRAWLING IMPLICATIONS

Democratization of Innovation

Mashups

Easily Modifiable Agile Development

Perpetual Beta

ERP End-Arounds

Semantic Web for Skeptics

TIM O'REILLY HAS A COMPREHENSIVE EXPLANATORY FRAMEWORK...

Web 2.0=Improvement Through Increased Use

EXAMPLES:
- Google's Use of Links
- Amazon Recommendations
- Flickr

COUNTEREXAMPLE:
- MapQuest

Core Patterns of Web 2.0

Key Attributes of Web 2.0: Massively Connected, Decentralized, User Focus

...THAT RAISES IMPORTANT QUESTIONS ABOUT HOW ENTERPRISE 2.0 MAY EMERGE

ERP with Network Effects

Call Detail Records: The Ultimate Social Network

Software as Service

The Platform API Divide

Barriers to Enterprise 2.0

Figure 2-1. Web 2.0 Chapter Map

In fact, Web 2.0 is as much a social phenomenon as it is a new stage of technical achievement. Indeed, the two go hand in hand, with one billion people worldwide enjoying some form of Internet access, hundreds of millions with always-on broadband connections, countless cell phones and other mobile devices connected wirelessly, and the Web increasingly woven into daily life as a tool for work, education, and play.

Given all that, it was no surprise that the International Research Forum's Web 2.0 session turned out to be the liveliest and most wide-ranging of the day. It touched on everything from Web 2.0's potential impact on the enterprise to the widespread use of scripting languages to the feasibility of the so-called Semantic Web, seemingly the next watershed in Web technology that some pundits already are calling Web 3.0.

In an effort to define Web 2.0 more precisely and to delve deeper into the topic, the authors of the present book invited as virtual forum participants **Tim O'Reilly,** head of O'Reilly Media and the foremost speaker on Web 2.0, and **John Musser,** creator of ProgrammableWeb. com, a web site that tracks the growth of Web 2.0–style web services platforms, and the myriad mashup applications those platforms are supporting, along with Dr. Peter Kürpick, an executive board member at Software AG. The contributions of the virtual participants help us build on the forum discussions and present a comprehensive explanation of Web 2.0. To conclude the chapter, we then examine more fully the potential that Web 2.0 has to change enterprise computing, a trend known simply as Enterprise 2.0.

Democratization of Innovation

As the session's first speaker, **Deependra Moitra,** Associate Vice President & General Manager (Research) at Infosys Technologies, put it, Web 2.0 represents first and foremost the "emergence of new value around the Web." What kind of value? Originally conceived as merely an "information dissemination system," the Web quickly morphed into a transaction platform facilitating ecommerce. And now, in the Web 2.0 era, it has morphed again into a platform for interaction and collaboration. This new mode of usage is the source of implicit and explicit value, for collaboration in the way of Web 2.0 is not solely the kind that individual users engage in when working together. To a degree that's unique in the history of IT, a true Web 2.0 application is the product of a rich, vibrant three-way collaboration that involves:

- masses of users

- the programmers who control the application's code

- most important, the applications and platforms themselves

"There is a democratization of innovation," Mr. Moitra explained. "We are able to harness collective intelligence from users as opposed to the previous one-way communication, from a provider to a bunch of users."

Understanding the full import of this shift requires a peek under the hood of Web 2.0. Its applications are delivered not as hard-coded binary files but in a form that is Web-based, scriptable, and brought to life with services—mutable, instantly updatable, centrally managed, and accessible anywhere a standard web browser is handy. These applications rely on the Web, not the desktop computer and its proprietary operating system, as their primary programming platform. As a result, these applications are shifting personal computing's center of gravity—the locus of program execution and data storage—away from the desktop and up into the Internet cloud and to massive datacenters.

Yet, even though they are delivered from remote locations and presented through common web browsers, these new applications give users virtually the same zippy, interactive experience that they've grown accustomed to in traditional software. That's made possible by sophisticated new programming techniques and swift, broadband connections. In short, Web 1.0's static web pages are giving way to lively, almost cinematic displays of text, graphics, and rich media.

What's more—and here's where that new form of collaboration kicks in—Web 2.0 applications are purposely built to be highly flexible and open to continuous evolution and modification. The most successful Web 2.0 creators have embraced lightweight, agile programming methods—component assembly and mashups of existing web services and high-level scripting languages, for instance—so that they can get new products to market quickly and then respond almost immediately to the emerging demands from users or to changes in business conditions.

 **Deependra Moitra** is currently an Associate Vice President and the General Manager for Research at Infosys Technologies, India, where he spearheads research and development on emerging technologies, directs intellectual property commercialization, and advises CXO-level executives on technology strategy and business innovation. Previously, he served as a start-up team member and general manager in Lucent Technologies' India R&D Centre, where he was responsible for managing multi-location, multi-cultural software R&D and product development programs. Prior to that, he held various managerial and technical positions in Siemens and Indian Space Research Organization.

Deependra regularly advises multinational companies and venture capital firms, serves on several advisory boards as well as journal editorial boards, and frequently speaks at various forums around the globe. He specializes in global innovation management, technology strategy and business innovation, management of emerging technologies, and services innovation. He is co-author of the book, "China and India: Opportunities and Threats for the Global Software Industry" published by Chandos Publishing (Oxford) Limited, 2007. He can be contacted at *deependra@moitra.com.*

"We have perpetual beta releases of software, as opposed to specific yearly or quarterly releases," Mr. Moitra said. And as hosted services, he explained, Web 2.0 applications can be maintained and modified in a single location, versus having millions of copies of a software package installed on millions of computers.

And, while Web 2.0 has mainly been used to describe blogs, wikis, and social-networking services, all of which thrive on users' direct contributions of personal musings, film reviews, photos, and other content, Web 2.0 thinking has penetrated into the enterprise, too. Blogs and wikis, of course, are catching on in many corporations as easy-to-install, easily mastered tools for knowledge management and workgroup collaboration. Even more promising, however, is the idea of getting traditional, core enterprise applications to harness network effects. By monitoring and analyzing their own usage patterns, meta-data, log files, statistics, and other usage-generated information, these applications may well be able to steadily improve themselves, Web 2.0–style, as well. They will gain value not only as perceived by individual employees but to one degree or another, by trusted business partners, too.

As Mr. Moitra sees it, applications compete on the basis of the experience they're able to deliver to customers. "Everything that we do on the technical front is really about how can we deliver better experiences to be able to compete," he said, and that calls for a "democratization and cocreation of experience. If I actually have to deliver greater experience to users, I need to understand what, for them, might constitute a great experience. There has to be, therefore, a democratic process so that this experience can be jointly created."

The Seismic Shift of Web 2.0

With this basic description of Web 2.0 sketched out, the International Research Forum session was opened to everyone's observations and critiques. **Michael Schrage,** Research Associate at the MIT Media Lab, kicked things off by looking at the changes Web 2.0 is fostering in programming methods and the relation between newly empowered users and their IT departments. He pointed, first, to the mix-and-match aspect of Web 2.0.

"What we are seeing in Web 2.0 are not just dedicated services or dedicated apps," Mr. Schrage said, "but the ability to fuse apps, to hybridize them, to mix them up. The fundamental paradigm shift is that we're accelerating away from the notion of software and systems as engineered and towards a model based on improvisation, iteration, and interaction-driven design."

A prime example, he said, are Google Map mashups. "The ability to take an app that looks interesting and stick it into another one has improved dramatically," Mr. Schrage said.

Meanwhile, a "less is more, keep it simple" philosophy permeates Web 2.0, Mr. Schrage said. Small teams design and build software

Michael Schrage is a Research Associate at the MIT Media Lab and a senior adviser to MIT's Security Studies Program. He advises organizations on the economics of innovation through rapid experimentation, simulation, and digital design.

A former director of Ticketmaster, Mr. Schrage advises its parent InteractiveCorp., a leading provider of online transaction services worldwide. He has been an advisor/consultant to such organizations as Accenture, Johnson & Johnson, MasterCard, Cisco, REI, Microsoft, British Telecom, BP, Mars, Fujitsu, and the Global Business Network. Mr. Schrage has presented invited papers on innovation economics for the Chemical Sciences Board of the National Research Council. He performs non-classified work for the National Security Council, the U.S. Defense Advanced Research Projects Agency (DARPA), and the Pentagon's Office of Net Assessment on command, control, and cyber-conflict management issues.

A columnist for *CIO Magazine* on IT implementation issues and "diffusion of innovation" management for MIT's *Technology Review* magazine, he serves on the editorial advisory board of the *Sloan Management Review*. He contributes op-ed pieces on national security and public policy to the *Washington Post*, *Wired*, and other publications. He's also written for the *Harvard Business Review*, *Wired*, *Across the Board*, and *Strategy+Business* magazines.

using agile methods; technology solutions build on simple data formats and protocols; software becomes simple to deploy with light footprint services built on open source software; business focuses on keeping investment and costs low; and marketing relies on viral, consumer-to-consumer referrals.

Mr. Schrage reckoned that this embracing of improvisational methods has profound implications. "What was good engineering is now perceived as over-engineering. And what is over-engineering is now perceived as a waste. Individuals and organizations have come to believe that immediate gratification takes too long. This, in turn, has moved us away from the notion of structured software development to what I would call the scriptification of software and the scriptification of process design, that is, the use of scripting languages such as Perl and Python—languages that didn't even exist until recently."

Mr. Schrage then raised the "very important issue" of users importing Web 2.0 services in ways that may "bypass or disintermediate the ERP." He stated that there has been a proliferation of what he termed soft processes. "Some people like the word 'agile;' I like the phrase 'cheap and easy to change.'" But the ability to change applications and processes so easily creates potential problems. As more people freely modify services and use mashup techniques and so forth, community-defined standards will take over from traditional, "people-think-hard-about-it" standards, and that, Mr. Schrage said, will lead to challenges in managing versions of code and services. Community-defined interfaces and standards, he said, may change as quickly as every 12 or 24 hours. "Amazon and eBay, not services to be ignored, have already been experiencing these kinds of issues," he noted.

In addition, he said, the economics of build-versus-buy are changing: "We're going to see more screen-scraping and the leveraging of what people are actually doing, as opposed to doing sophisticated gap-analysis and asking, 'what software can we build to fill the gap?' This leads to what I would call in the corporate environment, 'build your own ASP,' or BYOASP. In the same way we have bootleg web sites, we're going to have bootleg services and bootleg processes in organizations."

"I would wager," he added, "that if SAP were to audit some of its biggest clients, it would be pleasantly surprised—or perhaps quite shocked—by the level of bootleg processes that have been developed either to bypass or to supplant the main ERP processes."

One factor driving this build-it-yourself approach is the experience people have enjoyed for themselves on the public Web. "We've seen so much innovation on the consumer side of things," Mr. Schrage said. "People in the enterprise are looking outside and saying, 'Hey, if I can Google things externally, why can't I Google the structured and semi-structured information inside the organization? It really ticks me off that we're spending hundreds of millions of euros on an IT infrastructure, and what I get for free on Google seems more valuable to me.'"

More Critiques

Dr. Maria E. Orlowska, Professor in Information Systems at the School of Information Technology and Electrical Engineering at the University of Queensland in Brisbane, Australia, praised Web 2.0's notion of the "perpetual beta." Web 2.0 companies are selling services, not products, which means "there is no more hassle about the new shipment of the new release, there is no issue about compatibility. It's basically a continuous, even hourly, upgrade. There's no more waiting two years for a new release."

Dr. Orlowska identified a potential friction, however, that may arise between Web 2.0's laissez-faire attitude towards data and the traditional goal in enterprise IT of trying to lock down data and maintain its integrity and correctness at all costs. Web 2.0 applications, she said, involve the syndication of data: "sending data out without any concern or control over what server is involved or what will happen on the other end when the data actually comes to the connection point. There is not any provision for accuracy, currency, and integrity of such data sets. This is a very fundamental principle of the Internet, but it is a very relaxed requirement as far as data quality is concerned. It is fundamentally different from enterprise computing and typical business applications, where we are absolutely strict about correctness, consistency, transactionability, recoverability, trust, and many, many other features." And then there are purely technical issues as well—consolidating and maintaining the integrity of data pouring in from mashup applications is beyond the scope of existing database management systems, she said. "When we look at the data, streaming in from hundreds of millions of applications, current database technology will not be able to respond… the out-moded concept of data processing may not be really appropriate."

Prof. Max Mühlhäuser of the University of Darmstadt pointed to potential problems in using the Web as a platform on which developers would stitch together component services. "I'm a little bit frustrated as to where we've gotten with distributed components over the years. We had class hierarchies 25 years ago, we had some improvements in component technology led by Microsoft, but since then, all we did was to move these concepts into the Web."

The web services model, Prof. Mühlhäuser said, is simply a way of describing the interface syntax of the services we offer—a method now 30 years old. What's missing, he said, is a way of "really understanding the services out there, how we would combine them, orchestrate them. We should put an effort into making the Internet truly a free market, where you can deploy services, offer them in a competitive fashion, and compete against comparable services the way we run a free market in our economy. We don't have that in the Internet today." Crossing the barrier from widely available services to more easily understandable semantics is one of the key promises of the Semantic Web, the discussion of which concluded the session.

A Skeptic's Tour of the Semantic Web

Anyone looking for the *next* big thing on the Web—the next one after Web 2.0, that is—will quickly encounter talk of the Semantic Web. Already being referred to as Web 3.0, the Semantic Web is a compelling vision of where Web technology is headed. It centers on a simple proposition—namely, to make the Web's content understandable by computers, more or less unaided by humans—but realizing that promises to be anything but simple.

The Semantic Web was a contentious topic at the International Research Forum, drawing many skeptical comments. Elsewhere, the vision of a Semantic Web, full of computers interacting with each other autonomously, has spurred lots of technical research and entrepreneurial effort, lots of speechifying, lots of technologically minded speculation. Leading the way, all along, has been Sir Tim Berners-Lee, the man credited with inventing the World Wide Web while working at Switzerland's CERN high-energy physics laboratory. Berners-Lee actively promotes the idea of a Semantic Web and has contributed a good deal of technical insight and vision from which others have taken inspiration. Berners-Lee has described his thinking like so:

I have a dream for the Web [in which computers] become capable of analyzing all the data on the Web—the content, links, and transactions between people and computers. A "Semantic Web," which should make this possible, has yet to emerge, but when it does, the day-to-day mechanisms of trade, bureaucracy, and our daily lives will be handled by machines talking to machines. The "intelligent agents" people have touted for ages will finally materialize.

Not surprisingly, much controversy surrounds the Semantic Web, for it is not entirely clear how to make Berners-Lee's vision a reality. One issue is how to represent information and data in a way that computers can easily interpret and act on it—a longstanding problem in business computing and an even greater challenge when pursued on a global scale across the radically decentralized Internet and its millions of servers.

The deeper concern is the Web's original architecture, or the lack thereof. The Web was built, or authored, around pages of information that are intended primarily for viewing by the human eye. This leaves computers, when unaided by human intelligence, pretty much in the dark. The Web's HTML markup language merely describes where on a page specific blocks of text and graphics should appear. HTML determines the items' graphical relationships to each other but leaves it up to the intelligent viewer to determine and interpret any logical relationships that may exist between these items. A page that's labeled "catalog" and that provides a well-ordered list of products, specifications, and prices may be quite readable and useful to people seeing the page rendered in their browsers. But a computer given the same data underlying this graphical presentation might have great difficulty in making any sense of it. Without any explicit clues, or metadata, indicating exactly which products are listed and exactly which descriptions and prices are associated with which products, a computer might easily—and grossly—misinterpret the data.

The Semantic Web would overcome this problem by adding gobs of metadata to the Web's information. In theory, this metadata, expressed in specialized versions of the XML markup language, would provide contextual clues about the meaning, or semantics, of the data it embraces. And, in theory, this would make it possible for computers to make sense of Web pages—or entire databases, for that matter—that they had never before encountered. In other words, computers could roam the Web in search of data without having to be first introduced to each data source and given detailed information about the formats and information schemas that each one happens to be using. Moreover, computers could use this metadata to reason about the data they found—to make inferences and provide answers to complex questions. To cite a simplistic example, the Semantic Web one day might be able to point a shopper to the retailer who sells the model XQ-017 audio amplifier for the best price while also selling Klipsch loudspeakers, being located within 25 kilometers of a particular address, staying open until 9 p.m. on Tuesday nights, and providing an in-house warranty.

While considerable progress has been made in working out many low-level details of the Semantic Web, the concept has come in for a fair amount of criticism and doubt. Building the Semantic Web is an ambitious undertaking and it involves layer upon layer of new constructs and software schemes, and they won't work together as a whole unless everyone involved agrees to stick to certain standard interfaces and protocols. But as always, there are philosophical and technical disagreements about which of those to choose.

Discussion of the Semantic Web at the International Research Forum was not entirely rosy. Indeed, some serious doubts were expressed, mainly having to do with the Semantic Web's striking some participants as warmed-over artificial intelligence (AI). Leading the charge was Michael Schrage of MIT. He said he was "sympathetic to the goals of the Semantic Web and notions of understandability," but, with his own background in AI, he said "we should leverage what machines do well and leverage what people do well. One of the things that machines do well is not to be more like people. And one of the things that people do well is not be more like machines. It would be a mistake to try and rekindle the dying embers of artificial intelligence, to choose Web 2.0 as the platform for the next generation of AI research."

A key question for the Semantic Web is who will tag the Web's information so computers can interpret it. In his opening remarks, Mr. Moitra espoused his belief that "customers will be actually at the forefront of driving improved metadata" via tagging and the creation of "folksonomies," that is, ad hoc taxonomies created by the aggregation of individual tags. "There is obviously a need for improved ontologies, and obviously there are standardization efforts, but I think that's an area where work is needed."

"...we should leverage what machines do well and leverage what people do well. One of the things that machines do well is not to be more like people. And one of the things that people do well is not be more like machines."

Others believe that industry groups and other communities must work out standard sets of tags for their members, while others believe the tagging can be left to individual owners of data sources. Said one participant: "I'm a bit skeptical about the bottom-up approach of the Semantic Web, where a community would define the ontology or the semantics." He cited the Flickr photo site as an example of a community-indexed set of content. "This is really awful. I tried it. The annotation is so bad that you can't use it seriously. So I think it's really a business to design good ontologies." It's not the end user who will design these, but the software applications industry. Or, as another speaker reckoned, the music and film industry, which would benefit from making the content it owns more easily searched by customers. "Warner Bros., Universal, the movie studios—these are the guys who will design—with the help of the software industry—very good ontologies. When you use the bottom-up approach, relying on the community, it will be a semantic chaos." Then again, as Mr. Moitra also brought up, managing intellectual property rights in a Web 2.0 world is anything but settled. Viacom's public demands in February 2007 that YouTube (and by extension, Google) remove clips mined from its properties from the video sharing site only underscores how threatened rather than empowered media owners feel by Web 2.0 technologies.

Hewlett-Packard's **Martin Merry** saw the Semantic Web as "a collection of standards for building data models" that the modeling of a collection of data in a way that is independent of the application that created the data. "There is no AI, there is no magic, there is no getting computers to do things that humans are better in doing, it's simply a way of structuring information in a way that it's processible by more than one application. You need to add a level of semantics that can represent the constructs that the application used and then you can start to share those."

Yet another participant suggested that automatic metadata tagging should and will be built into the next generation of content design tools, which should help to improve the situation somewhat. "If the user edits a new home page or web site for his own company, we can design the editor in such a way that the semantic annotation is a kind of spin-off effect of the editing, so it's very easy. If you have such tools, I think the Semantic Web—I'm much more optimistic—will fly."

Dr. Nabil Adam, Professor of Computers and Information Systems at Rutgers University, said he saw "a lot of hype" about the Semantic Web. "We had the same hype with AI. We have to really come down to basics. There is nothing magic about the Semantic Web. One of the major components is ontology, and that is a challenge. There is a lot of work that needs to be done and it cannot be done by one organization, one business or industry. It has to be done in a distributed manner and there has to be technology to integrate. We have to go about it in a systematic way and not think of it as magic, but in terms of building blocks."

One solution to the semantics problem may be the one Google has come up with, rooted in an analysis of everyday language usage.

Peter Kürpick is a Member of the Executive Board of Software AG, having joined the company in April 2005. In his current role, he is responsible for the company's crossvision business unit, which includes research and development, product management, and product marketing. Dr. Kürpick started his career in IT in 1998 as a software developer and served as Senior Vice President, SAP, where he was responsible for major parts of the SAP NetWeaver stack.

"Semantics may be something that will happen through statistics and through the masses, instead of that very German way of sitting down in the back office and trying to define what the semantics of a certain topic could be," says **Dr. Peter Kürpick.**

According to Dr. Kürpick, Google has long been analyzing its users' search queries, in classic Web 2.0 fashion, to steadily build a large taxonomy of the terms that people are using to describe the world. Google freely shares this taxonomy with its customers to help them choose the search terms that will trigger Google's ad servers to present their ads on selected pages all across the Web.

"Semantics may be something that will happen through statistics and through the masses, instead of that very German way of sitting down in the back office and trying to define what the semantics of a certain topic could be."

For Google, he explains, this taxonomy "comes for free, due to all this enormous amount of search." Google just runs statistics on what people are looking for. And it can very quickly identify new terms and their meaning as they emerge in people's everyday lives. "It's happening by statistics, by the population, not by somebody sitting in an office and writing it down and then trying to push it out to the world, out on the street." This taxonomy is a valuable asset for Google and some day, he says, Google could use it to improve searches.

By indexing web content according to its taxonomy, Dr. Kürpick says, Google could speed searches and help people zero in on content according to its meaning.

"Maybe we should look at how language develops," Dr. Kürpick says. Taxonomies may not develop as well through academia as they do "on the street."

At this point, although the forum's participants had poked and prodded at all of the major body parts of Web 2.0, many more questions had been raised than answers proffered. While discussion about Web 2.0 will clearly continue for years, one clear takeaway from the discussion was that the concept is so broad and encompasses so much activity that it not easy to define. Tim O'Reilly and John Musser spent much of 2006 grappling with how to define Web 2.0, analyze its impact, and understand how to put it to work in businesses large and small.

In late 2006, Messrs. O'Reilly and Musser published a lengthy report, part of the O'Reilly Radar series, called *Web 2.0: Principles and Best Practices.* It identifies, describes, and analyzes eight fundamental characteristics of Web 2.0 and shows how Web 2.0 is reshaping the software business. Based on this report and interviews with both men, the rest of this chapter attempts to further define and explore Web 2.0 and its corollary, Enterprise 2.0.

Web 2.0 Examined

Web 2.0 may be many things to many people, but to Tim O'Reilly, founder and CEO of O'Reilly Media, it is a source of considerable pride. In 2004, his Sebastopol, Calif., company jointly coined the term Web 2.0 as the name for a technical conference. And ever since, Mr. O'Reilly himself has been at the forefront of interpreting this constellation of technological developments and its implications for startup companies, investors, and, increasingly, the mainstream enterprise IT industry.

Tim O'Reilly is the founder and CEO of O'Reilly Media, a publisher of technical books and journals headquartered in Sebastopol, Calif. The company also publishes online through the O'Reilly Network and hosts conferences on technology topics. Among these is the Web 2.0 conference, jointly produced with CMP Media. He is an activist for open source, open standards, and sensible intellectual property laws.

Since 1978, Mr. O'Reilly has led the company's pursuit of its core goal: to be a catalyst for technology change by capturing and transmitting the knowledge of "alpha geeks" and other innovators. His active engagement with technology communities drives both the company's product development and its marketing. Mr. O'Reilly describes his company as one where advocacy, meme-making, and evangelism are key tenets of the business philosophy.

Mr. O'Reilly earned his B.A. cum laude in Classics at Harvard.

As Mr. O'Reilly sees it, the core idea behind Web 2.0 is that "the network is the platform" and what distinguishes any true Web 2.0 application or service from others is that as people use it, it continually improves its results and usefulness. The true Web 2.0 application either directly solicits input from users—their personal photos, for instance—or it mines data and metadata that are automatically being generated by some underlying process. This

"...what distinguishes any true Web 2.0 application or service from others is that as people use it, it continually improves its results and usefulness."

is a direct consequence of its being a network-based application, Mr. O'Reilly says, and therefore able to harness so-called network effects.

Just as the value of each telephone on a phone network increases with the attachment of every additional telephone, so does the value of a Web 2.0 application increase with each person who joins its community of users. This network effect is easiest to see on the original Web itself: The more people there were on the Web, contributing content to it with new web sites and new web pages, the better the entire Web became for everyone. Next came blogs and wikis, the first applications to earn the Web 2.0 moniker. They were designed with the explicit intention of taking contributions from individual users, and with making it easy for them to do so. Blogs invite comments from readers; wikis freely encourage limitless additions to and editing of their content by visitors. Neither, of course, requires much, if any, training or technical know-how, yet they both can be set up to present their content as stylishly as required.

But the promise of Web 2.0 goes further than these early examples, Mr. O'Reilly argues, because network effects are at work, explicitly and implicitly, in a wide variety of existing and newly invented applications and services. And the big challenge for today's software industry is to identify opportunities where these effects are available for profitable exploitation. This challenge arises not only in the consumer-focused marketplace but in the enterprise software business as well.

Web 2.0 Application	How It Is Improved by Use
Google Search	Google's PageRank algorithm uses links to measure and prioritize search results. As the Web expands, so does the number of links, improving Google's search capabilities
Amazon Recommendations	The more customer data Amazon aggregates—in the form of purchase histories and items viewed on the site—the more accurate its product recommendations become
Flickr tagging	Users uploading photos automatically share them with the collective pool (but also have the option of making them private). In this way, Flickr aggregated the largest collection of photos on the Web very quickly. Users add tags for each photo, thus creating their own taxonomies for searching millions of photographs.

Google, eBay, and Amazon data centers	The computing power necessary to serve millions of search results, auction listings, or books for sale has resulted in giant platforms with tremendous spare capacity. Google, Amazon, and others have begun exploring how to use their platforms to deliver applications (such as Google Docs' online word processor) and resources (such as Amazon's hosting services) to consumers. The platform itself becomes a product and a competitive advantage.
MySpace and other social networks	A critical mass of users triggers the "network effect," in which the addition of each new user increases the value of the network exponentially. Social networks can quickly scale to unprecedented size, as MySpace and YouTube demonstrate. More specific networks, such as LinkedIn, rapidly aggregate colleagues and make previously invisible connections visible and useful.

Google's Community of Links

Mr. O'Reilly points to the Google search engine as a prototypical example of a large-scale application being engineered to take advantage of network effects. Ahead of their competitors, Google's founders saw that by analyzing the structure of hyperlinks that make the Web what it is, it would be possible to provide superior search results. Overlooked by others, these hyperlinks were actually a vast and highly valuable collection of data, all supplied inadvertently by millions of people as they published—and refreshed—their pages of content. Analyzed the right way, these links served as a sort of proxy, or voting process, that could be used to rank individual pages. More links pointing to a page indicated that more people had evaluated that page and found it worthy of linking to.

In essence, Mr. O'Reilly says, Google has mined the behavior of all its users and all the people on the Web. "They have all of these different mechanisms but what they are ultimately doing is not just purely algorithmic, working out the data of the documents—it is looking at the behavior of the network." The network, that is, of people creating the Web's content. Google is also able to evaluate how people use its search results and learn even more about the popularity and usefulness of web pages.

Network effects cannot be left to chance, however. They must be purposely built into applications, actively fostered, and aggressively used to good advantage, Mr. O'Reilly says. In short, the best Web 2.0 applications are designed to inherently exploit network effects, and the companies that succeed in this regard stand a good chance to be the winners in their respective markets. And, Mr. O'Reilly warns, those companies that don't rise to the challenge risk being displaced: "The applications that have not figured out how to do this will fail."

Amazon's Focus on Capturing Behavior

Mr. O'Reilly views Amazon.com as another example of successfully using network effects. Amazon started out with an unembellished database of all books in print. But to distinguish its book database from all others called for adding lots of unique content: customer-written reviews and ratings of individual books, customers' lists of recommended books, results of collaborative filtering that reveal which items get viewed or purchased together, and so forth. "They had to harness users in hundreds of different ways to make their database better than what they started with and better than the databases of their competitors," Mr. O'Reilly comments.

This harnessing of customer behavior has obviously worked. Amazon has made itself a major player in the book industry, and it is aggressively applying the same model in many other consumer markets and even certain industrial sectors. The company has not rested on its laurels, either; it steadily tries out new features that solicit user-generated content—wikis, lists of recommended books, and even a variation on the blog idea, which it calls a plog.

MapQuest: Stopping Short of Web 2.0

Mr. O'Reilly holds up AOL MapQuest as a counterexample, a company that missed an opportunity to do something similar with a market-leading database and has subsequently suffered at the hands of nimbler, Web 2.0–savvy competition. In Mr. O'Reilly's view, MapQuest eyed the navigating and presenting of online maps and driving directions "as an algorithmic or pure database problem." Google, in contrast, created a competitive map service and went the extra step of making its data and map images available for others to work with. Google did this by offering stable, well-documented programming interfaces that numerous individuals and companies have worked with to create a wide range of so-called mashups—services that combine two or more disparate sources of information into something more or less new. Thousands of mashups have been created with Google Maps (ProgrammableWeb.com maintains a current list) and while MapQuest is hardly a failure, it has lost considerable market share and mindshare to Google. Granted, some of these mashups remain essentially toys, but many successfully marry personalized and localized information to create an incredible bond with users. One of the most interesting (and occasionally terrifying) is a Google Map mashup hosted by the New York city blog Gothamist.com that combines real-time police reports with maps of the city. Nothing brings home the applicability of Google Maps like noticing a crime that literally happened just down the street. Mashups can also help with tasks like looking for a house in a particular part of a city, as is the case with HousingMaps.com shown in Figure 2-2. (Yet another mashup might combine these two ideas, offering a historical look at crime in an area as well as houses and apartments for sale or rent, providing a view of the safety of certain neighborhoods.)

Flickr Shoots Ahead

Likewise, the highly popular Flickr photo-sharing site—now a unit of Yahoo!—was able to quickly pull ahead of Ofoto, another photo site that enjoyed a five-year head start. Flickr was better at getting network effects going among all of its users, Mr. O'Reilly says, because its default setting made sure that "users' photos were shared with everyone else rather than kept private." This simple change meant that as more people uploaded their photos to Flickr, the whole of its content grew larger and richer in content and therefore more alluring as a destination for the general public. More viewers meant more subscribers, which meant more photos, creating a virtuous circle.

Figure 2-2. The prototypical mashup: HousingMaps.com offers a visual housing search page using dynamic overlays of Craigslist home listings on Google Maps

Flickr, it should be pointed out, has also encouraged—and greatly benefited from—tagging, another key Web 2.0 innovation. Flickr invites its users to categorize their images by making up their own keywords for individual items. While hardly perfect—inevitably, different people tend to categorize the world and individual photos of that world in different ways—the fact that these tags are user-generated makes them quite intuitive and easy. There's no need to learn a centrally defined set of categories, or formal taxonomy. Indeed, another term for these user-generated tags is folksonomies, reflecting their homegrown, vernacular nature. While this bottom-up, user-generated tagging falls significantly short of the sort of precise taxonomy that advocates of the Semantic Web are seeking, it still clearly provides significant value. Like many aspects of Web 2.0, it is fuzzy, imprecise, ever-changing, and good enough.

Consumer Software as a Service

Another compelling aspect of the Web 2.0 model is its delivery of software as an online service and here, Enterprise 2.0 may be closer to reality. Many enterprise software packages can now be ordered in service form. This appeals to the software maker as a way to reach new, usually smaller customers and it appeals even to large customers as a way to reduce IT expenses. As enterprises adopt the notion of SOA, more of their internal software functions will be delivered as remotely hosted services, too, and these in-house services may serve as components to be assembled, Web 2.0 mashup-style, with other services provided by third parties.

In fact, numerous startups have been launching Web 2.0 applications with a specific focus on the small enterprise. Their assumption is that small companies, with limited IT budgets, can make good use of online applications, even if they don't match corresponding desktop applications—frequently criticized as bloatware because they have accumulated so many options and toolbars over the years—feature for feature. The online applications provide the bulk of the functionality that most potential users need and use, and that's quite enough to build a viable company. In 2006, for instance, a small company called Upstartle launched an online word processing service. Considering that this service was presented for use entirely within a standard web browser, it provided an astonishingly rich and engaging interactive experience. It looked and felt, for the most part, just like a popular word processing program running natively on the PC. Later in the year, Google acquired Upstartle and renamed the word processor Google Docs. Google provides that service along with an online electronic spreadsheet program and a hosted email service—very successful among individuals and small businesses—called Gmail.

An outfit called 37Signals LLC, meanwhile, has hit pay dirt with an online project management application called Basecamp, a group real-time chat service called Campfire, and an information organizer called Backpack. 37Signals says these programs have attracted more than 1 million users. Its slogan: "Elegant, thoughtful products that do just what you need and nothing you don't."

As later sections of this chapter will describe in some detail, Mr. O'Reilly and others have strong ideas about how Web 2.0's core ideas will play out in the enterprise—what's come to be called Enterprise 2.0. In fact, it is precisely in the enterprise, many experts believe, that these ideas will have their most significant impact, and their usage will hardly be constrained to such simple and obvious applications as blogs and wikis being used to aid in what was once called knowledge management.

Web 2.0 Defined—For the Moment

In early 2007, O'Reilly Media published a report that defined and analyzed Web 2.0 and its implications for new and existing companies and for enterprise IT. Importantly, the report goes beyond simply describing the host of new applications and services that have hit the consumer-focused Web over the past couple of years—Flickr, MySpace, and del.icio.us, for instance. The report boldly predicts that these technologies will have growing importance within the enterprise computing scene, too:

> *While Web 2.0 has initially taken hold in consumer-facing applications, the infrastructure required to build these applications, and the scale at which they are operating,*

means that, much as PCs took over from mainframes in a classic demonstration of Clayton Christensen's "innovator's dilemma" hypothesis, web applications can and will move into the enterprise space.... Consumers' experience with Web 2.0–class software is setting the bar of what software can and should be. Consumers are bringing that knowledge, as well as those expectations, into their roles as corporate employees.... Web 2.0 is leading to Enterprise 2.0. CIOs and IT executives will only succeed if they are ahead of the curve through an understanding of the workplace benefits and challenges of Web 2.0. The differences in needs and culture "behind the firewall" mean adapting external models to the appropriate internal ones. Enterprises can learn from consumer Web 2.0 lessons, such as massive scaling, capturing network effects, and creating rich user experiences.

The O'Reilly report goes on to identify several key attributes that support these eight patterns. To begin with, Web 2.0 applications are **massively connected:** Network effects create a true web of many-to-many connections that replace the one-to-many publishing and communication models of the past. Now, the edges become as important as the hub, and old modes of communication, publishing, distribution, and aggregation are disrupted. Web 2.0 applications are also **decentralized.** Connectedness disrupts traditional control and power structures, leading to greater decentralization. Bottom-up now competes with top-down in everything from global information flow to marketing to new product design. Adoption occurs via pull, not push. Systems often grow from the edges in, not from the hub out.

O'Reilly's report cites the **emergent** quality of Web 2.0 applications. With agile software development and assembly techniques available, it's not necessary—or even advisable—to work up a full list of strictly defined requirements when developing a new software product. Instead, the code can evolve according to the agile development paradigm, which recommends small interactive steps, each one

Core Patterns in Web 2.0

The O'Reilly report sees eight fundamental ideas—or "core patterns," as software design professionals would say—as fueling Web 2.0. These core patterns are depicted in Figure 2–3.

Harnessing collective intelligence. Services harness an "architecture of participation" that encourages masses of users to directly contribute content or supply implicit data. Then, unique algorithms can use those contributions to steadily improve the service's function and utility. Example: Amazon.com's ecommerce site, rich with users' product reviews and Amazon-generated recommendations.

Recognizing the value of data. Unique, hard-to-duplicate collections of data are becoming as important to a service's success as its logical function. In many cases, this data is provided by users themselves, in the form of personal photos and web pages, restaurant and product reviews, and even remixed music tracks (for example, JamGlue.com). In other cases—Google's analysis of web hyperlinks, for instance—the data is collected from indirect sources.

Innovation in assembly. Service platforms can be designed specifically to enable the rapid remixing of data and services such as mashups, which can help companies to quickly address fast-emerging business opportunities.

Perpetual beta. By delivering software as a service, it can be updated as frequently as necessary, with no worries about incompatibilities with other software on the desktop. Example: Salesforce.com, delivering a range of enterprise IT applications as online services.

Rich user experiences. Static web pages are obsolete, now, as users expect dynamic, interactive Web content and access to rich media like video. All this is made possible by new combinations of desktop and online software—Ajax, Flash, and Ruby on Rails, for example.

Pervasive computing and access. Web 2.0 services must accommodate the growing range of mobile devices that, thanks to nearly ubiquitous wireless access, are able to remain online virtually 24/7. Example: Yahoo!'s mobile services.

Leveraging the long tail. The Internet's broad reach and low cost make it possible for businesses to serve niche markets that in the past were often too small to bother with. Examples: Amazon selling books and NetFlix renting DVDs. Titles with narrow appeal can still be found by a small but significant audience.

(continued on next page)

(continued from previous page)

Lightweight models and design for scalability. By using lightweight business and software-development models, it's possible to jump on fleeting market opportunities, gain first-mover advantage, and scale a Web 2.0 business rapidly and at relatively low cost.

---

taking into account the latest feedback from customers and the marketplace. Software design isn't dictated up front; it emerges over time. A flexible, adaptive strategy permits appropriate solutions to evolve in response to real-world usage; success comes from cooperation, not control. Ideally, usage directly improves the application's function.

The report also notes the **user focus** in Web 2.0. The user is at the center of Web 2.0 and has gained unprecedented power for participation, conversation, collaboration, and, ultimately, impact. Consumers have become publishers with greater control, experiences are tailored on the fly for each user, rich interfaces optimize user interactions, users actively shape product direction, and consumers reward favored companies with loyalty and valuable word-of-mouth marketing.

Frontiers for Enterprise 2.0

The key shift required for Enterprise 2.0 thinking is to understand how to maintain the integrity of the hub systems, which record the core transactions of an enterprise, while at the same time using that data as the foundation for learning and improving the behavior of applications. Enterprise 2.0 means letting go of rigid notions of control in a way that leads to increased value, not chaos.

According to Mr. O'Reilly, the biggest opportunity for enterprises to exploit Web 2.0 lies in introducing network effects—and in turn, the capability for self-improvement—into their own enterprise software.

"The really interesting frontier," says Mr. O'Reilly, "is how to get network effects out of systems where the people don't even know that they are participating and they don't necessarily have to be actively doing anything to make these effects take hold." The prototype for this kind of

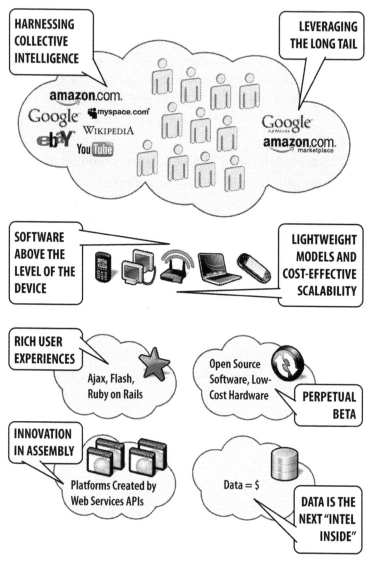

Figure 2-3. Eight core patterns of Web 2.0, as identified by John Musser in
Web 2.0: Principles and Best Practices, *an O'Reilly Radar series report*

thinking is the Google search engine, he says: The search engine doesn't schedule massive analyses of the data it's constantly collecting. Instead, the search engine is continually adjusting itself in real time, as it collects new data, and users can benefit from its improvements immediately.

Playing at Work

The Internet is widely considered to be both the greatest boon to productivity in the history of the world, and also the greatest time-waster ever invented. Beginning with email forwards and tracing an evolutionary path through Napster, blogging, and YouTube, the Internet has shattered attention spans and transformed some employees' working hours into a one giant Web surfing session. As it turns out, that may have been a good thing.

The explosion in mashups and APIs freely available on the Web has left many organizations and their developers in a quandary: how can they possibly evaluate the potential uses and value of each one without playing with them? So in many cases, that's exactly what they've done. Many Web 2.0–savvy individuals channeled their time-wasting impulses into "playing" at work, making testing new APIs and mashups an integral part of their daily tasks, without any overt agenda. Google, of course, was the first and most famous to do this by mandating that its employees spent 20 percent of their time working on blue-sky personal projects, and others have had the same realization that serendipity and brainstorming can produce powerful tools or even new lines of business. After all, Google's own mashups were born that way.

Data and ERP 2.0

While much of the discussion surrounding Web 2.0 has focused on consumers contributing bits of personal content to some widely shared database—book reviews on Amazon.com, videos on YouTube, and so forth—enterprise applications may benefit from the automated collection of implicit data from throughout a company's operations. Statistically analyzed and mined, this continuous stream of fresh data could yield valuable insights and lead to new efficiencies. Properly conceived, hub applications could be set up to improve their effectiveness over time, quite automatically.

Mr. O'Reilly urges enterprises to focus on their data assets: "What data assets do you have that you are using in this old mainframe way, so to speak, with massive, project-based data mining taking place every so often? Can this be changed to Web 2.0's live behavior, with the application being continually informed and improved by user activity?" For example, keeping track of which help screens users view most often can identify the screens that are most confusing.

IT managers, he suggests, must ask themselves, "what data could we share that would make this system grow organically and get better the more people use it?"

He points to ERP systems as a possible beneficiary of Web 2.0 thinking. "If we start from the premise that the network is the application—that the network is the platform—how would we build a better ERP system? You would build one that was smart because of its connected data suppliers."

Such an ERP system could be made to improve itself by collecting information from all of the facilities whose operations it is overseeing and optimizing. The various IT systems up and down the supply chain, Mr. O'Reilly explains, could act in the same open style as a Web 2.0 consumer application. The self-improving ERP system would be one that used Web 2.0 principles in the relationship between its components, each of which would be set up to communicate about itself. "The better supply chain would be the one with more information shared, with more connected warehouses and factories and more alternate paths to get a particular component from A to B."

As Mr. O'Reilly sees it, "an RFID-enabled warehouse is promiscuous in the same way that a Flickr data store is promiscuous. It is reporting about itself continuously." In both cases, the systems share data widely, with anyone who asks, opening up the opportunity for unanticipated use of that data.

Web 2.0 concepts can be useful in quite unexpected circumstances. In New York City, Mr. O'Reilly points out that Swedish cellular equipment maker Ericsson in late 2006 won approval for plans to install wireless sensors in some 50 Yellow Cabs. As the taxis roam the city's streets, the sensors identify wireless dead spots, which operators can then try to ameliorate by boosting their signals there. Says Mr. O'Reilly: "It is a fabulous example of how the taxicab passengers are the random route generators ensuring complete coverage of the city. Neither the passengers nor drivers know they are participating, but the system as a whole has been instrumented to become a useful part of Ericsson's application."

In some companies, data that has been kept private may actually be a valuable asset. Phone companies, Mr. O'Reilly notes, are sitting on vast troves of call data that, viewed the right way, describe a good portion of each subscriber's social network—not only the people he or she calls on the phone, but data about how often each one gets called and how long the resulting conversations last. "Can you imagine if your phone had an address book that was built on Web 2.0 principles?" Mr. O'Reilly asks. All companies, he urges, need to look at the transactional data they have on-hand and ask, what metadata is that data embraced by that the company could mine to make it more useful?

Loyalty programs are another area ripe for Web 2.0, he says. "Enterprises could take their relationship with their customers and make it smarter in the same way that Google made search smarter."

Collaboration

Certainly, the enterprise seems ready for at least some parts of the Web 2.0 model. One of the most important aspects of Web 2.0, for instance, seems to be its emphasis on collaboration, and anyone who knows corporate life knows that enterprises thrive on collaboration. Individuals and groups of people are constantly having to share information, coordinate schedules, attend meetings, work with others to create complex action plans, and so forth. Might some new form of collaborative software be of help?

Needless to say, countless past attempts at supporting collaboration with various forms of automation have more or less failed compared with Web 2.0 variants. Just look at all the companies launched under such promising labels as knowledge management, workflow automation, coordination technology, and collaboration itself. Some of these schemes involved quite sophisticated modeling of human interaction, language, and intent; others simply applied keyword filtering. In the end, as it turns out, email and, to a degree, instant messaging—and lately, wikis and blogs—have succeeded best in helping far-flung workers and workgroups to coordinate their calendars and share documents. These tools have succeeded precisely because they fit the Web 2.0 model: they are lightweight, easy to master, and massively scaleable.

Will Web 2.0's version of collaboration—fairly unstructured and decentralized—be of any use in the enterprise? Judging by the increasing popularity of wikis and blogs, used internally and as ways to stay in touch with customers, the answer is a definite yes. Numerous executives at brand-name companies now blog, publicly and for their colleagues' consumption, though the benefits of this may be mainly in the form of good public relations. Microsoft has permitted—and perhaps even encouraged—some of its top technologists and managers to blog, and their freedom to criticize their employer has only boosted their credibility.

Collaboration takes many forms. For years, many producers of complex high-technology products have benefited from setting up online bulletin boards where their customers can, in effect, collaborate by posting questions and answers and searching for tips and advice. These online communities not only save manufacturers money by getting problems resolved with less use of costly call centers, but they also foster a certain intimacy with and loyalty from important customers. Some product companies are using blogs and wikis to establish communications between their own developers and those outside the company who seek to work with the products' public APIs or even produce unauthorized extensions.

What other kinds of explicit collaboration might be aided by Web 2.0–style computing is difficult to say. On the one hand, for workers in an enterprise, time is money, and, in theory, anything that helps them save time and become more efficient in executing work tasks and coordinating their scarce time with others would seem to hold strong appeal. On the other hand, beyond wikis, blogs, and RSS feeds, other styles of Web 2.0 applications that could help with enterprise collaboration are only starting to emerge. The decentralized nature and emergent structures of Web 2.0 are, in a way, antithetical to traditional

IT, which sought to impose top-down control on data to maintain its integrity.

Enterprise Software as a Service

The model of offering software as a service offers both advantages and disadvantages from a tactical point of view. In the software-as-a-service paradigm, software vendors offer access to their software online, typically for a subscription fee. However, delivering their products as a service is not something that all software companies will want to get involved in themselves. Achieving the levels of reliability and responsiveness that customers will demand requires major investments in datacenter infrastructure. But some producers of software may be able to take advantage of others' software delivery platforms—to piggyback their wares on those of an established software-as-a-service provider.

For example, the eBay platform is serving many companies, too, as a relatively low-cost but global ecommerce sales channel. Thanks to the APIs eBay makes available, companies can list their goods on the auction site fairly easily, without having to navigate through eBay's hierarchy of web pages. What's more, eBay's PayPal unit can collect and transfer payments to merchants, and its Skype unit provides Internet-based telephony services through which shoppers, in some cases, can speak directly to merchants.

Software as a service is just one way to expose software functionality as services. For many companies, putting sensitive corporate information in the hands of a third-party hosting provider is not acceptable. But the drive toward Web 2.0–style service enablement is just as strong for those companies and the need for flexibility and using APIs to extend to new markets and rapidly create new applications is just as great. Using what it calls enterprise service-oriented architecture (enterprise SOA) as an organizing principle, SAP is adding services to all of its applications and publishing those services in an Enterprise Services Repository, which is the foundation for the creation of composite applications. In this way, applications that are installed and run at a company can also benefit from the power of services.

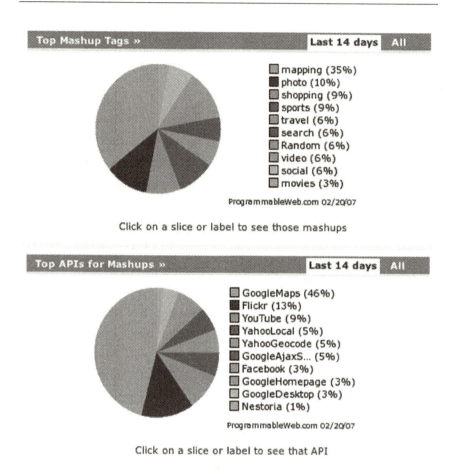

Figure 2-4. Top mashups and APIs listed on ProgrammableWeb.com

SAP has also changed the way it releases its SAP ERP 2005 to take advantage of the potential of service enablement. Rather than bundle more and more features into new releases of ERP, SAP has declared that SAP ERP 2005 is stable until 2010. To add improvements to this hosted product, SAP embraced SOA at a fundamental level, exposing the core functionality of its software through enterprise services. So twice a year for the next few years, SAP will release new collections of services based on SAP ERP 2005 in what are called Enhancement Packages. Each Enhancement Package contains groups of solution-oriented services referred to as enterprise services bundles. In this way, SAP provides gateways to existing functionality so that ERP can be extended and new applications can be developed.

To help developers with this fundamental shift, SAP continues to enhance its SAP Developer Network (SDN), which itself exemplifies a Web 2.0 application with its focus on the user, emergence, and perpetual beta. SDN hosts a thriving community of developers who collaborate using blogs, forums, and wikis.

SDN hosts multiple wikis, but one wiki of note is the Enterprise Services wiki, which documents the services in each enterprise services bundle and helps developers collaborate on and work with these solutions. Through the Enterprise Services wiki, developers can read about scenarios where enterprise services can be deployed to solve particular problems and can drill down into the Web Services Description Language (WSDL) for individual services. Developers can then contribute their code back to the wiki, modifying its content to reflect their experience in working with the services.

SDN takes a multimedia approach to supporting developers, with e-learnings, webcasts, and blogs aimed at the hottest development topics. A thriving community has developed that is so active that the average time it takes to get an answer to a question posted in a forum is 15 minutes. Since Web 2.0 is affecting the enterprise in fundamental ways, enterprise software must be adaptable. SAP's strategy with enterprise SOA and SDN embodies this idea.

The Platform Divide

Many of the questions that most companies will have to ask themselves as they grapple with the forces driving Enterprise 2.0 concern on which side of the platform divide a company will find itself. Some companies are natural platform providers, which will find access to new markets and streams of transactions through designing and releasing web services APIs. Other companies are natural consumers, which will benefit from becoming expert in putting these APIs to work.

John Musser is the founder of Programmable Web.com, the online resource covering mashups, APIs, and other topics relating to the Web-as-platform. He is a Seattle-based technology consultant, writer, and teacher. During his 20-year career in software development, Mr. Musser has shipped five award-winning software products in three industries working with companies including Electronic Arts, Credit Suisse, MTV, and Bell Labs. He has taught at Columbia University and the University of Washington, and he has written for a variety of technology publications on the topic of software development.

Thinking that Enterprise 2.0 is still a thing of the future ignores the success many companies have achieved by presenting their wares through platforms constructed of web services APIs. While eBay Inc. may never have adopted the term Web 2.0 per se, that company is arguably the first and still the most important provider of a Web 2.0 platform—a highly reliable, globally available, well-documented services platform on which the rest of the industry has been formally invited to build new applications and services.

According to Mr. Musser's ProgrammableWeb.com site, approximately 25 percent of all the listings that eBay currently presents on its electronic auction site are there not via a traditional eBay web window, but via other applications and services communicating to its systems via a public programming interface. "There's an entire ecosystem of people who've built tools, who've built web sites, who've built this entire infrastructure around eBay auction listings," Mr. Musser says.

Amazon.com is another major provider of Web 2.0 platform services, moving aggressively to leverage its web-based computing assets. Most people are familiar with its affiliate program, which enables any web site to display an Amazon "Click here to buy this book" ad and pass click-throughs to the retailer in return for a share of any revenue generated by a sale. According to Mr. Musser, about 180,000 developers are working with the programming interfaces that make that program work, building tools, applications, and web sites that feed traffic to Amazon. Over the past couple of years, however, Amazon has begun offering more or less "raw" computing resources—mass data storage capacity, high-performance high-reliability processing, and so forth—to all comers. Says Mr. Musser: "Much to many people's surprise, Amazon is providing the new infrastructure—pieces of a web operating system. Now, you can run your entire web site on Amazon," taking advantage of its years of experience in running large datacenters and making services available at high volume and with high reliability.

The Challenges of Enterprise 2.0

Surely, Mr. O'Reilly lays out a compelling vision of Enterprise 2.0, but corporations have a good deal of work ahead of them before they'll be able to turn that vision into reality.

Many challenges lie in the way of fully realizing the promises of Enterprise 2.0. Its technologies are, in many ways, antithetical to traditional IT. For instance, these technologies seem to yield the greatest benefits when they are applied in a fairly unstructured way and users are encouraged to mix and match them, to experiment and to mash different resources together. As Web 2.0 services evolve, moreover, their behaviors may emerge in unexpected, unpredictable ways, which is in stark contrast to the detailed planning and hard-coded functionality of traditional applications. Where Web 2.0 would have a thousand flowers bloom, in hopes that a few of them will catch hold and thrive over the long-term, traditional enterprise IT has looked for ways of exploiting and controlling homegrown, "shadow IT" initiatives, sometimes trying to stamp them out altogether.

Unfortunately for the control-minded CIO, many of his or her company's employees already are exploring and relying on Web 2.0 at home, and it's only a matter of time before they begin to insist on using their favorite Web 2.0 services at work, too, because these services help them do some task better than officially available tools. This is hardly a new phenomenon—think how wireless nodes were stealthily attached to many corporate local area networks so that individuals could enjoy the same wireless freedom with their laptops that they were enjoying at home. It's a safe bet that with or without IT approval, Web 2.0 applications and services will find their way into the enterprise.

As more individuals grow accustomed to Web 2.0 in their off-hours, they will likely find some of the legacy enterprise applications they use in the office pale in comparison: less interactive, less engaging, less personalized. (How many of us miss the quick search of Gmail when we are using MS Outlook and other email clients that lack this capability?) In time, these Web 2.0 experiences will prompt users to demand changes in legacy systems and the introduction of Web 2.0, a.k.a. Enterprise 2.0, concepts in the systems that their IT departments provide. (Google was early to identify this phenomenon and to directly exploit it. With its search engine so popular among individuals, the company has designed its enterprise search appliance to present an identical user interface. That keeps training costs down and makes the system friendlier and more intuitive to enterprise users.)

Barrier: Development Skills

How well corporations will be able to create their own Web 2.0 applications and services, however, is a big question mark. The easy services, such as blogs and wikis, have been done and are available either as open source projects or as for-profit commercial products. That leaves the more sophisticated applications, which enterprises may well identify as particularly useful and worth developing in-house.

But there's a problem: As truly engaging and cleverly crafted as many Web 2.0 applications are, with their rich, dynamic user experiences produced within standard browsers, building such applications remains quite challenging. Some observers estimate that currently, only 2,000 developers or so in the entire world are capable of building the most advanced Web 2.0 applications because such projects require strong competence in several highly specialized constructs such as Ajax and Ruby on Rails. And many of those developers aren't eager to work for large corporations. Thus, it may be some time before run-of-the-mill IT departments can turn out Web 2.0–style applications of similar sophistication.

Without question, enterprises can, and should, take steps that will better position them to benefit from ongoing Enterprise 2.0 developments such as adopting standards, trying out open source toolkits and technology stacks, and experimenting with lightweight software assembly models. It's a good idea to try out a few of the commercial Enterprise 2.0 services, too, to see how they work and what they're capable of. For an in-house development team, simply working with an application that remains in "perpetual beta," for instance, may be just the kind of inspiration needed to spur a homegrown project in the same vein.

Barrier: The Large-Scale Data Center

Web 2.0 services won't do away with the client PC as we've known it for 25 years, but they certainly have the potential to greatly diminish the worth of that machine and its internal components—its microprocessor, its richly featured operating system, and its sizeable hard disk. Web 2.0 applications arrive over the Web, delivered as services hosted in far-off, large-scale datacenters. Those same datacenters also store the bulk of the data that these applications use and generate. For this reason, Web 2.0 is a disruptive force in the software industry, opening opportunities for relative newcomers like Google to wrest market share and control over key interfaces from traditionally dominant players like Microsoft. Indeed, Google and Yahoo! have been buying up promising Web 2.0 companies, such as YouTube and Flickr, to better position themselves in this critical stage of competition.

As the locus of computing and storage shifts from the client device up into the cloud, Google, Yahoo!, and Microsoft, among others, must scramble to build out their datacenter infrastructures. Reliable numbers are difficult to come by, but widely published reports estimate that

Google now operates around 600,000 servers around the world. In 2006, both Google and Yahoo! were reported to be planning massive datacenters fairly close to each other in Oregon, mainly because the cost of electrical power is relatively low there. Power consumption and cooling have become key considerations in the location and design of these large-scale facilities, and everyone, from Intel Corp. and Advanced Micro Devices Inc. supplying microprocessors, to IBM and Hewlett-Packard producing servers, is investing in ways of slashing power consumption.

On the one hand, enterprises may find it difficult to scale up their own datacenters as they seek to implement Enterprise 2.0 systems. Running even normal-sized datacenters efficiently has become a stiff challenge. On the other hand, managed datacenter services are widely available from various specialist firms. As mentioned, too, Amazon has begun selling computing and storage capacity in its own datacenters, a move that other Enterprise 2.0 companies may follow if only to leverage their investments.

Barrier: Letting Go

Perhaps the largest barrier to Enterprise 2.0 is psychological. There is a leap of faith in almost every aspect of Enterprise 2.0 in which a company must let go of control to achieve the benefits. If you create an API and publish it for use, you don't know how it will be used. If you change a system so that it improves based on captured data, the usage patterns will change the system in ways that you cannot anticipate. If you unleash collaborative systems into a population of workers, their thoughts will start to emerge, whether you want them to or not.

The idea of emergence is friendly to those who expect that the more people are involved in something, the more value is created. Traditional command and control structures are at war with this concept. While Enterprise 2.0 concepts are in their infancy, it is clear that each side of this debate will have powerful arguments.

The participants at the **International Research Forum 2006** took a forward-thinking yet balanced view of the potential and the challenges facing Web 2.0 and its implications for Enterprise 2.0. Participants highlighted the importance of the democratization of innovation, which harnesses the collective intelligence of users, of the perpetual beta, and of mash-ups with mix-and-match components that can support malleable business processes for speedy adaptation to changing market conditions—all of which are essential elements for the transition to Enterprise 2.0.

IT Security

It was October 19, 2006. Internet Explorer 7, Microsoft's venerable Internet browser and flagship product, was ready to launch. After months of beta-testing, tire-kicking, and praise by the tech press and users' groups, the browser became available to everyone around the world.

In the world of software development, a program like Internet Explorer is a true three-ring circus. Designed to work on almost every PC built from 1999 onward, Internet Explorer 7 had to meet the expectations of a mass audience in ways that most programmers cannot imagine. Internet Explorer 7 had to be better than the much-maligned Internet Explorer 6—Microsoft's user base and stock price was counting on it—and as the program spread through the Internet everything looked perfect. The new version included tabbed browsing, a feature well-established in other browsers and long missing in Internet

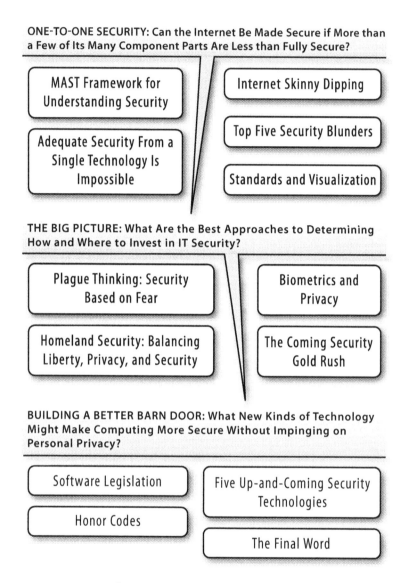

ONE-TO-ONE SECURITY: Can the Internet Be Made Secure if More than a Few of Its Many Component Parts Are Less than Fully Secure?

MAST Framework for Understanding Security

Adequate Security From a Single Technology Is Impossible

Internet Skinny Dipping

Top Five Security Blunders

Standards and Visualization

THE BIG PICTURE: What Are the Best Approaches to Determining How and Where to Invest in IT Security?

Plague Thinking: Security Based on Fear

Homeland Security: Balancing Liberty, Privacy, and Security

Biometrics and Privacy

The Coming Security Gold Rush

BUILDING A BETTER BARN DOOR: What New Kinds of Technology Might Make Computing More Secure Without Impinging on Personal Privacy?

Software Legislation

Honor Codes

Five Up-and-Coming Security Technologies

The Final Word

Figure 3-1. IT Security Chapter Map

Explorer, as well as a plethora of security improvements that ensured that this release would be a solid, useful tool for millions.

Within the first 24 hours, Internet Explorer 7 was compromised. An unusual bit of code could reveal private and potentially valuable information about any user and enable a "phishing" attack—a method of faking a web site to make it appear genuine.

Microsoft spent six years and countless man-hours building, testing, and debugging Internet Explorer 7. A dedicated band of user/testers attempted to crack it from all sides and reported thousands of errors while teams of programmers costing millions of dollars hammered out multiple issues and tried to produce the most secure browser on the market. They immediately, and spectacularly, failed.

If juggernauts like Microsoft can't keep their software secure, how, then, can a small IT company—underfunded, understaffed, and overwhelmed—expect to survive?

Security has always been a vitally important issue in the field of IT, but with the rise of the Internet, social-networking, and wireless networks, the issue of security has grown in prevalence and importance. Virtually every computer is now connected to every other, and the people using those computers are being encouraged at every turn to share files and information with complete strangers. Securing individual computers is much more difficult when they are connected to and able to receive malicious code from potentially millions of other machines.

The key to Internet security is staying one step ahead of the bad guys. But how? The **International Research Forum 2006** discussed the rising need to maintain and implement secure systems and began the discussion by asking a few very important questions in the face of these threats.

One-to-One Security

What does security expert **Dr. Pradeep Khosla** of Carnegie Mellon University want? It's simple, really.

"Give me a completely secure networking infrastructure and computer system," he said, opening the International Research Forum's IT security session with a quip about the impossibility of complete and total system security.

"You will never build a system that's 100 percent secure."

"It's easy for people to talk about 100 percent security," Dr. Khosla said. "It's easy for politicians to talk about it. But technically, you will never build a system that's 100 percent secure."

**Pradeep Khosla** received a Bachelor's Degree with honors in Tech from Indian Institute of Technology in Kharagpur, India, in 1980, and M.S. and Ph.D. degrees from Carnegie-Mellon University. He is currently Dean of the College of Engineering, Philip and Marsha Dowd Professor of Engineering, and Founding Director of CyLab at Carnegie-Mellon. His previous positions include Founding Director of the Institute for Complex Engineered Systems (ICES) and Program Manager at DARPA.

Dr. Khosla's research interests are in the areas of reconfigurable and distributed collaborating autonomous systems, agent-based architectures, reconfigurable software, and security for embedded and distributed information systems.

Dr. Khosla is a recipient of several awards, including the ASEE 1999 George Westinghouse Award for Education, Siliconindia Leadership award for Excellence in Academics and Technology in 2000, and the W. Wallace McDowell Award from IEEE Computer Society in 2001. He is a Fellow of the Institute of Electrical and Electronics Engineers, the American Association of Artificial Intelligence, and the American Association for Advancement of Science. In 2006, he was elected to the National Academy Of Engineering (NAE).

Dr. Khosla currently serves on the editorial boards of *IEEE Spectrum,* and *IEEE Security and Privacy,* and the Oxford Series in Electrical and Computer Engineering, and was appointed in 2003 to the National Research Council Board on Manufacturing and Engineering Design.

Dr. Khosla's research has resulted in three books and more than 300 articles. He is a consultant to several companies and venture capitalists, has served on the technology advisory boards of many start-ups, and is a cofounder of Quantapoint Inc., a high-tech company based in Pittsburgh.

From these inauspicious beginnings, Dr. Khosla began to describe the MAST framework. MAST stands for Measurable, Available, Secure, and Trusted. This is the baseline requirement of any system, on or off the Internet. This framework describes the ideal computing environment in any situation and highlights the various tradeoffs required to build a device that survives simple attacks, maintains individual privacy and security, and whose performance is easily quantified. The question, then, is: Is this device MAST-compliant and, if it is not, what aspects of the framework must be improved to ensure compliance?

Security, according to Dr. Khosla, is a multitechnology discipline, a methodology that is quickly moving beyond stand-alone secure devices into the very protocols and systems that make up the Internet.

Whereas once the main culprits were Windows machines infected by viruses and worms, the strength of antivirus and spyware software, coupled with a rise in Internet usage, makes completely new attacks considerably more virulent than anything cooked up by a fourteen-year-old in his or her bedroom.

"A few years back," said Dr. Khosla, "it was common to hear people complain about computer viruses and worms, and they always blamed one thing—a certain operating system from an obvious company."

"Security is a multitechnology discipline, a methodology that is quickly moving beyond stand-alone secure devices into the very protocols and systems that make up the Internet."

The mantra, even a few years ago, was "Blame it on Microsoft." But this view of IT security overlooked the fact that the threats are myriad and that many different technologies are required to provide reasonable and effective security. "There is no notion of any single technology making anything secure—it's not going to happen," Dr. Khosla said.

The key to the MAST methodology is assessing the tradeoffs necessary to secure a system. Security, at its core, is about taking educated risks. While a gambler wouldn't see his trade in the implementation of firewalls, the IT team makes daily decisions regarding their current level of security—which ranges from "free-for-all" to "lock-up-the-machine-and-throw-away-the-key"—and the risks they are taking by setting their alertness to any specific level. Go too far to one side and you end up "skinny dipping," a term popularized by well-known

 **Bill "Ches" Cheswick** was Chief Scientist for Lumeta. Ches worked for nearly 30 years on operating-system security, including 13 years of service at AT&T/Lucent/Bell Labs where he began his now famous Internet Mapping Project. The technology used for this project became the genesis of Lumeta.

An internationally acclaimed expert on security, Ches cowrote the bible for firewall management, *Firewalls and Internet Security: Repelling the Wily Hacker,* first published by Addison Wesley in 1994. His depth of knowledge has resulted in his being a frequent consultant to government agencies and an advisor to law enforcement for high-profile computer crimes.

Ches left Lumeta in September 2006 and is currently a free agent.

security expert and author **Bill Cheswick** (a virtual participant in the conference), which describes a machine completely outside of a firewall running a few dedicated, robust tasks that should, in theory, withstand any and all attacks. Go too far in the other direction and the system is unusable. How can the accounting team use a bookkeeping application when it's locked in an underground vault, unplugged from the world?

No one aspect of MAST is more important than the others, but when building a secure system, we must remember that 100 percent security is impossible and that security—like many other risk-taking endeavors—is expensive and resource-intensive.

The key to security is the mitigation of risk. Expensive solutions are useless if they open a service up to hackers and malware due to bugs and errors while inexpensive solutions—removing the Ethernet card, for example—create unusable devices.

Before we delve any deeper into the MAST framework, however, let's take a closer look at some of the threats as well as the methodologies for making something MAST-compliant in the industry today.

MAST

Measurable, meaning an outside observer must be able to measure the performance of the environment at any time using common tools.

Think of a boiler with a thermometer and a pressure gauge. If either—or both—of those measurement tools were missing or broken, the boiler would be a danger and all but unusable. Yet many firewalls and servers sit quietly in stuffy closets with no communication to the outside world. By the time an alarm is raised, the system is usually compromised beyond repair.

Measurable also equates to a measurable monetary gain—or a reduction of expenditures in a device. An insecure machine is a money pit. When it becomes compromised, the investment avoided at the outset becomes multiplied a thousandfold, as preparation is considerably cheaper than on-the-spot repair and forensics. The basic question is: "How much is this data worth and how much can we spend to protect it?"

Available, meaning a device won't die under attack. This is key to fending off attacks and performing forensics. Being "available" isn't just a matter of not crashing spectacularly. There are a few questions to ask about any high-performance, highly important server:

- Has load testing been performed to prevent local access and maintenance under heavy fire?
- Has a "pull-the-plug" protocol been put into place to remove the device from the network?
- Is the device backed up regularly and backups kept in multiple safe locations?

Secure, meaning a device is protected from intrusions and denial-of-service attacks. While this can never be truly tested, has the device been maintained and updated regularly? Do the administrators understand the device and its various failure points? What is on the device and how can that information compromise the organization or the network?

Trusted, meaning a programmer or user can be absolutely sure that a resource is just what it purports to be. The rise of web services and object-oriented programming has created a whole new class of servers. These servers offer data on an ad hoc basis, process information, or send out security clearances to other servers on a network. But what if that server is compromised or—worse—spoofed. How will outside programmers and administrators know that a device is really what it claims to be?

Internet Skinny Dipping:
A Discussion with Bill Cheswick

Cheswick: Internet skinny dipping is what I call working on the Internet without a firewall. It has the aspects of skinny dipping, which is that it is a little bit dangerous and, you know, maybe a little bit exciting. If you have no firewall protecting you then you are dealing with raw host security, which ultimately ought to be our goal. Every machine out there has to be fully resistant against attacks on the outside and I have been doing this for over ten years for most of the machines I work with. There are some that run services that are too fragile and they are protected, but the idea is, of course, that you run machines that offer no services to the outside world except ones they absolutely have to and those services are believed to be robust. But of course the one problem with skinny dipping machines is that they can be flooded with denial-of-service attacks. If that happens, you have to go do some sort of mitigation or move them or something in order to avoid it or suppress it or just wait them out.

Interviewer: What's the benefit of Internet skinny dipping?

Cheswick: Well for one thing, you get the full benefit of Internet features providing the services work. You can run a variety of clients. You can offer new services without having to poke holes in firewalls—and performance is so much better. You get peer-to-peer sorts of things that are not just file-sharing. You know the whole Internet was sort of designed to be peer-to-peer. Everyone was intended to be a peer with everyone else and you could invent new services. As soon as you set up a firewall, and I did this very early on, you then have to say what services am I going to let through, are they safe? You are constantly evaluating new services for safety and cost effectiveness. This can get in the way.

Interviewer: When would a company want to try skinny dipping?

Cheswick: The reason you would want to do Internet skinny dipping is if you have a machine that is so robust that you are confident that outside attackers can't break in. Once you have that sort of security, if you put it inside your intranet you don't have the crunchy outside and soft chewy center. You have a rugged center. You are dealing with robust things. What we are trying to do here is engineer secure systems with insecure elements. And of course, improving the security of these elements increases the layers, increases the security of the whole thing. Defense in depth has always been a good thing.

(continued on next page)

(continued from previous page)

Interviewer: I see.

Cheswick: So if you design these various services with Internet skinny dipping in mind, then you are making a more robust service even if that isn't where it finally deployed. Of course this also addresses the insider threat. It is all very nice to put up a castle wall but the traitors inside are still a problem and you want resistant machines on the inside that give you a better handle there.

Rogues' Gallery

Today's threats are becoming more network-based. Whereas many viruses and worms depended on host files to infect systems, denial-of-service (DoS) and port-sniffing/cracking are far more dangerous to the average computer user.

Dr. Khosla further pointed out that many of the technologies discussed at the forum are, by their very nature, vastly expanding the scale and scope of the IT security problem. Emerging applications like social networking, information sharing, online payments, and globalized workforce management systems are all placing a great deal of faith in a system that can trace its genesis to the heady days of the early 1960s.

"Sensor networks are reaching into every nook and cranny of an organization's facilities," Dr. Khosla said. "As a result of this great expansion in nodes on the network, security is going to change from purely computer-based and OS-based to large-scale, IT–infrastructure-based." (See the discussion of security concerns for sensor networks in Chapter 4.)

Denial-of-Service: Public Enemy Number One

As the forum progressed, participants could agree on one thing: denial-of-service is the most prevalent—and frightening—type of attack on the Internet.

Denial-of-service, or DoS, is an attack involving the use of a server's scarce resources. These resources can be anything—an incoming web connection, a server-to-server communications channel, or even disk

Top Five Greatest Security Blunders

Pentium III Serial Numbers. In the heady days of the dot-com boom, hardware and software manufacturers were trying almost anything to make online sales and security as easy as clicking a button. Enter Intel's Pentium III. The chip had a built-in "serial number" that uniquely identified the processor and allowed software makers to design security applications keyed to single processors. The outrage that followed was deafening as privacy advocates lambasted the chipmaker for putting identifying fingerprints on every PC. The concept was quickly shelved.

Trusted Computing Platform. Microsoft led the charge in this complex system for securing everything on every PC—the monitor, the CPU, and even the operating system. The concept was compelling: the Trusted Computing Platform prevented unsigned and unauthorized code from running on any computer. In reality, the intricate dance between hardware, software, and encryption was almost impossible to control and implement. The initiative is still hanging around but it is all but dead in the real world.

Digital Rights Management Rootkits. In a misguided effort to control access to their music CDs, Sony created a secret program that spied on music listeners and hid itself almost completely from standard antivirus and antispyware software. The software, discovered in 2005, allowed hackers to gain access to infected computers. After a thorough investigation, Sony began recalling the CDs and issued a public apology.

Closed Source Voting Systems. In an effort to "secure" its voting machines, Diebold closed and hid the source code to its high-end machines. After an anonymous whistle-blower posted the code online, however, programmers found bugs and security holes galore. After a few attempts to stifle the source code, Diebold finally decided to stop sending out its army of lawyers and instead began fixing its software.

Pay-per-Piece Email Systems. In 2004 AOL and Microsoft decided to start selling stamps for email. Never bought any? Don't be surprised. The idea was simple: charge bulk mailers for the ability to send millions of emails to unsuspecting recipients. Can't afford the stamp? Then don't send the emails. A solid idea in theory, but unworkable in practice and quickly abandoned.

space filled with bloated log files. While viruses, worms, and bombs fit into their own dedicated niche in the pantheon of system attacks, the term DoS can easily be expanded to describe any manner of attack. For example, spam is a DoS attack because it uses up an organization's scarce resources—bandwidth, disk space, and patience, to name a few—and is extremely difficult to prevent due to the nature of the Internet and email protocols.

Dr. Khosla pointed to DoS as perhaps the most important aspect of IT security today. "Building systems that guarantee no denial-of-service is a big thing. We can look at our computers as a service that is being given to us; computing is a service. We might own our computers, but still, it's a service that they are providing."

How does one build systems that can guarantee no denial-of-service?

According to Dr. Khosla, "That is a very different question than 'How does one build systems that are guaranteed secure?' because we can imagine a system that has software bugs and other sorts of loopholes, that has worms and viruses, all coexisting with honest, good code. Yet, at the same time, our service is not being denied. That is what we expect the system to do, and I think that's where we should be headed" as a goal in developing security technologies.

DoS attacks cannot be prevented but their effect can be reduced or rerouted. This is considerably more difficult than we first imagine, however, because of the current state of the Internet. Think of a DoS attack like a flock of migrating geese flapping over your freshly washed car. Individually, anything that might fall from their number is no concern—a nuisance, but nothing that the hose can't get rid of. In tandem, however, their attack can make a whole day's work come to naught and potentially condemn you to hours of cleaning and polishing.

Unfortunately, many DoS attacks come from massive botnets of zombie machines, ensuring that IT directors cannot just shut down one set of IP addresses and be assured another thousand won't suddenly pop up for an attack. The only method around this is an improved

---

Botnets: The Zombie Threat

Botnets consist of a networked group of computers working in concert to achieve a nefarious goal. Botnets usually use viruses or worms to embed a privileged program into a network PC, and hackers can then "contact" those programs through common chat or web protocols. Once a computer is part of a botnet, it becomes a slave to a distant master. Botnets can be designed to grab important files from infected PCs and even work in concert to create DoS attacks against specific targets.

---

and streamlined forward-facing web infrastructure that is completely separate from mission-critical internal applications.

A single attack on a port is a leaky window, a signal to batten down the hatches. A multiple-sided, multipronged attack is a deluge.

What can solve the DoS dilemma? Dr. Khosla believes that diligence and applying the MAST framework to devices is often the best—and only—recourse for many IT shops.

The Problem of Standardization

While DoS is a rising outside issue, think about the "measurable" portion of the MAST framework. To be "measurable," a human being must be able to understand and use a tool. However, human attention is finite and human understanding is limited. Systems, from PCs to nuclear reactors, rarely fail because of a missed warning. Instead, they begin to fail because there were too many warnings going off at once.

To that end, forum participant **Dr. Nabil R. Adam,** of Rutgers University, proposed that the second biggest enemy to security is lack of standardization.

"Time is of the essence," Dr. Adam said. "We can't say, 'give the user three minutes and let him go through the information until he finds what he needs.' Obviously, that's not going to work."

So, it's imperative to think in terms of human-centric support systems—systems that would effectively support decision makers that are dealing in a real-time, ad hoc manner with such activities as to protect, detect, prevent, respond, and recover.

Dr. Adam cited several critical technology issues. Semantics technology, he said, can help to improve discovery and search processes and help with the association of different pieces of information, perhaps gleaned from disparate sources, so that they can be more readily accessed and processed.

"What happens now," he explained, "is that when an incident takes place, a human sits there and, depending on the location and many other factors, he or she determines which agencies ought to be involved. There are already some semantics there, however, that make it difficult for the human to do that. What we would like to see is the machine helping out more with those decisions—machine-to-machine interaction in terms of automated and dynamic selection, composition of services, and monitoring services—so that we can achieve a certain goal."

Ontology—a way of simplifying a complex system by codifying it to a high degree—will be a critical element here, Dr. Adam said. "Here, we are talking about integration, maintenance of domain-specific ontology, as well as interrelated ontology." Ontology in the context of security means to reduce component parts of a security situation into something easily understood and implemented by a small team of programmers. This is the codification of the MAST paradigm, where each level of security is described using the simplest language possible.

Ontology allows for the merging of complex organizations and systems with a minimum of overlap and miscommunication. It can even improve communication between IT teams and their secure devices, among first responders, and between systems themselves. By translating the words "Help me!" into a language multiple systems can understand, the person, organization, or device in peril can be sure that its message is heard.

"There are lots of data being collected, so data mining is another challenge that we need to think about," said Dr. Adam. "That will help us to reduce the number of false positives and also help us to distinguish between malfunctioning sensors and a fusion of sensor data that

Dr. Nabil R. Adam is a Professor of Computers and Information Systems at Rutgers University in Newark, New Jersey. He is the Founding Director of the Rutgers University Center for Information Management, Integration, and Connectivity (CIMIC); Director of the Meadowlands Environmental Research Institute; and the Director of the Laboratory for Water Security.

Dr. Adam has published numerous technical papers in such journals as *IEEE Transactions on Software Engineering, IEEE Transactions on Knowledge and Data Engineering, ACM Computing Surveys, Communications of the ACM, Journal of Management Information Systems*, and *International Journal of Intelligent and Cooperative Information Systems*.

He has authored and edited 10 books, including *Electronic Commerce: Technical, Business, and Legal Issues*, a book on database issues in GIS, and one on electronic commerce.

Dr. Adam is the cofounder and the Executive-Editor-in-Chief of the *International Journal on Digital Libraries* and serves on the editorial board of a number of journals, including the *Journal of Management Information Systems*, the *Journal of Electronic Commerce*, and the *Journal of Electronic Commerce Research and Applications*. He is also the cofounder and past chair of the IEEE Technical Committee on Digital Libraries.

Dr. Adam's research work has been supported by over $15 million from various federal and state agencies, including the National Science Foundation (NSF), the National Security Agency (NSA), NOAA, the U.S. Environmental Protection Agency, the Defense Logistics Agency (DLA), the National Institutes of Health, the New Jersey Meadowlands Commission, and NASA.

covers actionable alerts, not just alarms—actual alerts that you can respond to."

Visualization: Keep It Simple

Further expanding on the idea of simplicity, Dr. Adam brought up the concept of visualization in ontology.

"The sensor network, so many thousands of sensors deployed in different places, is multimodal, so how can we make the sensor network more intelligent so that we are able to translate high-level semantics to low-level sensor parameters, such as the coverage, such as the location, such as the frequency of alarms."

What this means is that anything—from a network of computers reporting an attack to a collection of water-testing buoys bobbing in a reservoir—produces lots of noise. The real key is to "visualize" this noise and create a picture that is easily readable by humans and devices alike.

"Visualization technologies can help workers to grasp important information quickly and accurately," he said.

These systems involve XML and data warehouses that collect and store massive amounts of information that can then be fed into special templates that match each application for each first responder. Rather than seeing a mass of information, each template shows only what is necessary at any one time and avoids data overload.

Methods for sharing information securely will be crucial, too, and they'll have to be adaptable to accommodate the different makeups of emergency response teams. "The nature of a team may vary from one instance to another, given the cause of the incident. If it started in New York and then spread to New Jersey, policies may require other agencies, like public health and others, to join in." To help cope, distributed access-control models must be in place that can enforce policies for fine-grained access and select dissemination of information—"only specific information that I'm willing to share with the fire department, or with the health department. Secure information sharing is an interesting challenge."

The Big Picture

Now that we've discussed some of the worst culprits in the war against secure devices, let's look at some real-world examples of security in action. To do this, the forum participants opened the floor to **Claudia Funke,** Director in the Munich office of McKinsey & Company.

 **Claudia Funke** is Partner in the Munich office of McKinsey & Company. She leads the firm's German High-Tech Sector, which serves the software and services, datacom, consumer electronics, industrial manufacturing, and aerospace and defense industries.

Ms. Funke works primarily for industry leaders in software, IT services, and telecommunication in Europe and North/South America. Her main areas of expertise include:

- Go-to-market approaches: Increasing value capture from telecommunications and IT investments in complex solution environments, global account development, and outsourcing.
- Strategy/executive counseling: Corporate strategy, changing go-to-market models, innovation in high-tech, pricing, definition of strategic and operational turnaround programs, and coaching of executive groups.

Ms. Funke has led McKinsey's global knowledge initiative, "Serving Enterprise Customers: The Winning Formula for ICT Leadership," as well as most recently a major initiative about the future of the high-tech sector in Europe.

Before joining McKinsey Ms. Funke received an M.S. in physics from the University of Cologne. She served as a teacher at the university's department of theoretical physics and math and also worked as a professional dancer.

Irrational Thinking

Ms. Funke recounted an interesting anecdote from history that describes the problem of real-world security.

"The history of mankind has demonstrated that an irrational perception of threat will lead to irrational security procedures," she said. "For example, in the Middle Ages people were very much afraid of the Black Death. Now, in some regions, a rumor spread that the 'Pest' was caused by people painting fences black. As a result, the fence painters as well as their neighbors who had observed them and the observers of those observers were put in jail for interrogation. And as you can imagine, the interrogation techniques of the Middle Ages led to confessions that the actual cause for the 'Pest' was the fence painting."

Liberty and Safety Revisited

Governments, Ms. Funke said, can easily fall into a similar trap. "If a state invests more and more money into security to protect the freedom of its citizens, it risks losing both in the end—the security and the freedom."

"If a state invests more and more money into security to protect the freedom of its citizens, it risks losing both in the end—the security and the freedom."

The danger of irrational thinking threatens discussions and practice in IT security mitigation, too, she explained. McKinsey & Co.'s own experiences in the field have yielded three main lessons, Ms. Funke said: "First of all, investments in IT security should be assessed from an economic, business-case point of view. In some industries—the financial industries, for instance—investments in IT security have actually improved margins, by as much as 0.5 percent. But in manufacturing industries, for instance, several business cases have not been positive."

The second lesson concerns IT architecture. "From McKinsey's point of view, the best thing is to invest in an architecture that provides cost-effectiveness and flexibility. This means a streamlined application security architecture, which follows a services-oriented paradigm and has identity management at its core."

Finally, she said that the most effective risk mitigation levers are those that address IT and human behavior in parallel. An example: When an employee leaves a company, for whatever reason, "we've seen that there is a certain risk that the employee will intentionally disclose customer-confidential information to others or make massive downloads from the company's knowledge database. In addition to IT measures, the most effective measure is to communicate very clearly to the exit employee the consequences they face for misusing this proprietary information."

So, Ms. Funke concluded, "for corporate and public security, I would recommend taking a rational, business case–driven approach and considering measures that take into account both technology and human behavior."

Homeland Security Issues

Dr. Adam also shifted the panel's attention to homeland security—specifically, the challenges of facilitating and coordinating the sharing of critical data within an ad hoc group of disparate law enforcement and government agencies as they jointly respond to a major emergency.

"These agencies are at the federal level, state level, city level, and local level, and each of them is a consumer and a provider of information," Dr. Adam explained. "This is an environment where information must be shared, but in a secure way. It's an interesting challenge."

This ad hoc community of agencies is particularly diverse in several ways, he explained. "One, in terms of the services and content they provide and in terms of vocabulary. When different agencies talk to each other, it's almost as if they're speaking different languages." The technology resources each agency has at its disposal—bandwidth, databases, knowledge, connectivity, and so forth—vary widely, too. Finally, they will inevitably wish to share many types of data: text, images, sensor measurements, audio, and video, for instance.

These concepts clearly tie into the problem of standardization and visualization. When one organization can't hear another's cries for help, failure is imminent. Interestingly enough, when visualization fails and the ontology breaks down, one organization's constant, erroneous cries for help might be taken as false alarms.

"That's the way to rob a bank," said Mr. Cheswick. "Set off the alarm and wait for the police to come. Do it again. Do it a few more times. Finally, when the police don't come, the bank is yours."

Privacy Issues

"Privacy is a very big deal," Dr. Khosla said without irony. Protecting privacy is increasingly something that calls for a new class of technology that has to be developed in parallel. Successful use of biometrics, for instance, requires the collection and storage of much highly personal data, and to make sure that this data is kept private and unavailable to misuse in turn requires the development of a new class of technology.

"A simple example is a knife," Dr. Khosla says. "I first invent it to cut my meat or bread with, but then, you use it to kill somebody. That doesn't mean I should not develop the knife. Likewise, it doesn't mean I should not be collecting data about you."

Governments and organizations have to keep ideas of privacy near and dear to their collective hearts. Various examples of medical records being thrown away, intact, into public garbage cans, and laptops being stolen containing lists of Social Security numbers, are only some of the ways that security foibles can end up destroying trust and public acceptance of further security measures.

According to security experts Utimaco, in 2005, U.S. businesses reported 100 significant data security incidents, including stolen laptops, lost or stolen media, and security breaches, that exposed personal information of nearly 56 million individuals. Companies like Safeway, Marriot, Scottrade, and Bank of America lost media and laptops containing customer data or suffered security breaches that exposed customer information. Given this state of affairs no wonder Dr. Khosla foresees the need to build systems that protect the protected data.

"Similarly, I now must develop technologies that would assure my privacy even when people steal certain data, such as a biometric database," he said.

"Many of these databases with personal data are put together in a dumb manner. In a single file, they may have my name, Social Security number, birth date, and driver's license number. You can imagine this information distributed across multiple databases. You give one of them the name 'Pradeep Khosla' and it provides my Social Security number. Another service gives you my driver's license. But because this data is distributed, stealing from one of the databases doesn't enable you to get all my data in an easy manner."

Dr. Khosla said that medical records databases are a bigger problem.

"Even though the databases are more or less distributed, they must be proven to maintain an even higher level of security. Say there's a distributed database containing all of your medical records. And suppose that I'm allowed to make 10 different types of queries on this database to find out your name, when you had a disease, the medications involved, the doctors, and so forth. The owner of that database must be able to prove that there is no combination or sequence of these 10 queries that enables anyone to obtain information that they are not supposed to have. They should never be able to connect your name to a disease you had, for instance. They might query the database and say, 'Tell me who all had common cold in the last three months,' but it should never be able to say, 'Oh, Dan had this disease,' or 'Dan took this tetanus shot.' These are called privacy-preserving databases."

Dr. Khosla brought up another critical issue: "guaranteeing privacy with security." Unfortunately, most discussions about privacy, he said, have focused on lost credit card numbers and the like. "What we are not seeing as privacy issues is where I may be openly sharing information, not even thinking about privacy, yet I still have some hope that my information is kept private. This may actually be an oxymoron. On the one hand, in a social sense, I'm sharing my information, but on the other hand, I'm expecting it not to be shared beyond a known and trusted recipient."

Trust in computer and communications systems also demands special attention, Dr. Khosla said, "but what are the technologies or challenges? Imagine a network infrastructure that guarantees no denial-of-service. Cisco and Juniper might not be happy about that—or maybe they would, because it would require changing our whole networking infrastructure in the next 5 to 10 years—routers and everything—and that means billions of dollars of investment have to be made."

Biometrics and Privacy

Biometrics, Dr. Khosla said, promises to be a big issue, "again, closely tied to sensitive issues of privacy." In theory, biometrics could help stop hackers, but difficult legal and policy issues could easily arise.

"Part of the reason that it's so difficult to catch online criminals is that there is no notion of IP traceback. If we had networks with total IP traceback—computers where you are mandated to have biometric authentication 24/7, so that every second you're online you're being authenticated—we would have the ability to not only track the computer, but even the person who was using the computer," Dr. Khosla said.

Could the world accept such a system? Would you, a lowly computer owner, accept that in order to buy from an online store or view a friend's online photo album you would have to slide a finger over a scanner? Probably not, but a multipart authentication protocol could use biometrics as one part of its security system.

Biometrics, it seems, is proving to be a useful security measure when it comes to stand-alone hardware. With the threat of laptop and pocket-PC theft, a biometric security system, coupled with encrypted drives and a system that "wipes" a device if too many attempts are made to hack it, is the easiest and fastest way to maintain security. Passwords can always be cracked, but biometric security is considerably harder to break.

Is biometrics—or anything—the answer to our privacy questions? No. But the concepts are solid. Take for example Intellink, a system laid out by the NSA, designed to offer "Google-like" searching of top secret data. Mr. Cheswick posited that "it is a useful exercise to envision the policies and approaches one would use to design such a network where there is an extra high priority on getting the security right." Such a system has to have security built into it from the beginning, almost down to the hardware level. Advances in processing speed and power along with enhanced security methods can make systems like this a reality.

Data Mining and Real-World Sensors

Ms. Funke pointed out a real-world example of privacy butting up against the world of security. She cited the merging of video surveillance with biometric databases as an example of this convergence.

In Switzerland, she said, cars driving into a certain tunnel are filmed. The video is transmitted to a central processing center where a quick algorithm identifies the car by license plate number and matches it against a list of stolen vehicles. "When they match, that information gets transmitted immediately to the local police, and if they act quickly, they can actually nab the stolen car at the end of the tunnel. Which, by the way, shows the advantage of Switzerland, because they do have very long tunnels."

Ms. Funke noted that Swiss authorities have worked with Unisys in testing facial-recognition technology for identifying previously known hooligans when they show up in crowds at sporting events, for instance. "When they started, the recognition rate was 20 percent," Ms. Funke said. "That rate has since increased up to 80 percent, and since this experiment has been so successful, it is being applied in several Swiss nightclubs, as well."

Tools like these, using real-world sensors to capture real-world criminals, put a face to pie-in-the-sky images of security and, in another sense, bring privacy issues to the forefront.

But this sort of power requires investment, which brought Ms. Funke to her next point.

The Gold Mine

Looking at privacy and security is useless if you don't look at the overall cost of highly secure systems. Digressing from the idea of real-world applications, Ms. Funke began to discuss the economics behind the scenes of every security decision. She caught the forum's collective attention with her statement that "the security industry is a gold mine."

"The U.S. homeland security budget increased from $22 billion in 2002 to $40 billion in 2005. In 2004, the expenditure on security during the Olympic Games in Athens was 13 percent of the overall budget, compared with 5 percent back in Atlanta back in 1997. And last year (2005), the overall physical and IT security industry was around $200 billion. It's a big gold mine."

Driving this growth, Ms. Funke said, is "the perceived increase in threat" and four technological trends: "substitution, convergence, a reshuffling of services with medium complexity to high-end and complicated integrated services, and low-end, plug-and-play solutions." The latter she attributed largely to the entry of low-cost, China-based producers into the global marketplace.

Security is a business, replied Fabio Colasanti, but isn't it a difficult business opportunity? Ms. Funke disagreed.

"From a business point of view, investments in security could be an opportunity, definitely, or a protection against a threat. But whatever you do, there should be a clear business case behind it and you should look at the end-to-end process. This is not a fundamental conceptual problem but, with most companies we have worked with, an execution problem. The discussion starts deep down in the technology department, concerning the availability or the degree of security of an IT solution. From our perspective, that is just one piece of the overall solution."

The MAST framework is a tradeoff, and part of that framework requires it to be measurable. What is more measurable than dollar signs on a balance sheet?

The "money question" is fast becoming the largest topic looming over the security equation. While no one wants to lose data or face due to a massive break-in or failure, no one wants to spend huge amounts on what could end up being a false road. The real question, then, is how organizations can decide when and where their spending stops and the real value begins.

"From a public, homeland security point of view," Ms. Funke said, "I think it's also a conceptual problem, and much more difficult. What you would need there is a public discussion, political and social, about the benefits, the risks, and the costs affected by this. And when it comes to security, the degree of irrationality is high, so this dialogue is quite difficult to have."

Ms. Funke suggested that large IT providers—such as SAP, Microsoft, and Oracle—along with consultancies, have an obligation to simplify and streamline the security process. "We need to bring certain insights to the political decision-makers in an understandable way and then to make sure that we get something of a more rational discussion going," she said. "Even if we could get some cross-country collaboration around standardization, that would be a first big step."

The participants then discussed the inability of any device, no matter how simplified, to be completely secure, especially in a governmental context. The real concern was the tradeoff between application security and overall application performance.

The participants also pointed out that the increasing emphasis on flexibility and agility in IT architectures is affecting the security of IT systems. Whereas large-scale security projects were once the norm, small, more nimble projects are now cropping up, leading to a mismatch in priorities.

Many Hands Make Light Work

Although it is a frightening prospect, heavy-duty servers can also be easily attacked using lightweight and seemingly innocuous systems. For example, the participants also discussed machine-to-machine mobility. As a network device—a phone, a computer, or a security system—travels from place to place, it has to hand off its network functionality to cells along the route. The best example of this could be an armored car that is in constant contact with a central headquarters. Because the car is using a form of cellular communication to download updates and upload information, it can be tracked at a moment's notice. This means that anyone with the wherewithal to hack a cellular network can route the truck to any location without having to fight against the potentially heavy security. This "meta-hacking" means that hackers can move further down the chain—to your very infrastructure—rather than attacking the main systems.

Ms. Funke, however, was undeterred. She believes the dialogue is open and must be continued. "If you want to have a dialogue on benefits, risks, costs, and on the overall end-to-end security chain, then we, the IT industry, need to explain the important, critical issues to political decision makers."

Building a Better Barn Door

Cowboys don't save money or face by catching the cows that got away. They build better fences to begin with. It is this concept that drove the final discussion on how to follow the MAST framework. The forum participants began by commenting on the strategy of holding software vendors and governments responsible for producing software and systems that ensure security and privacy.

Software Legislation

The idea that good software can be legislated is not a new one—it's actually done all the time in requests-for-proposals between federal governments and software vendors. However, can companies hold to legislated requirements? "Is it a good idea?" Dr. Khosla asked, "Is it possible?"

Europeans are familiar with privacy legislation that states that everything—from your address to your shoe size—is privileged information. In fact, data mining, in the traditional sense, is technically illegal, which means European companies have to find creative ways to match customers up with their spending habits, for marketing purposes.

Dr. Khosla disagrees with this in theory. "I personally think it is a bad idea," he said. "If I ask people 'Is antispam legislation a good idea or a bad idea?' what would they say? It's a good idea. But actually, it's a bad idea because it creates a false sense of security."

It is this irrational thinking—something has been legislated and is therefore secure—that puts many companies and organizations at risk.

"By creating antispam legislation," Dr. Khosla said, "I have done nothing because there's no way of enforcing it."

The real goal, then, is to create better tools to prevent offenses and track down offenders. While federal or state investment could be in order, this process is time consuming and expensive.

Dr. Khosla sees legislation as faulty simply because there is no final way to prove it is working. "There is no way of proving with a 100 percent guarantee that a certain piece of code has no bugs, unless it's a very small piece of code, like 1,000 lines, and even then, only for a very small class of bugs, like buffer overflows."

Without being able to prove a device is bug- and error-free, how can we even begin to legislate security?

The Code of Honor

But legislation doesn't have to be the only way software vendors are liable for their wares. Liability is often written into provider contracts, yet how does it affect the bottom line?

Dr. Khosla believes that software liability—that is, holding vendors responsible for security in their products—is an idea that should spread far and wide in the industry.

"As soon as software producers become liable, the ability to guarantee that people are using the same software that you gave them is going to become of paramount importance," he said. "That is going to be a very big challenge. Very, very few people are looking at it right now, but it is an area we should focus on."

Bill Cheswick points out that such an approach may have unintended consequences. "Do we really want juries to decide whether a piece of software is secure enough? How would you educate such a jury about the intricacies of software design, the difficulty in testing and proving software, and the widespread effects even a single character typo can have?"

Against Overwhelming Odds

Forum speaker **Prof. José Luis Encarnação,** Professor of Computer Science at Technical University Darmstadt, lent a bit of humor to the proceedings with a story from the days when bureaucrats and secret police attempted to control the population in Eastern Europe.

"We have a joke in Eastern Germany," Prof. Encarnaçáo said. "The secret police had almost one security officer for each person in the population. So why didn't they succeed in controlling the population? In the end, it was because they had more data than they could filter and analyze. They didn't know how to handle so much data. And if I look at the homeland security problem, I get a little of that same feeling. We are collecting and sensing so much data that we now have a new problem, which is becoming a new discipline: visual analytics."

Prof. Encarnaçáo continued, saying that complex problems required simple, elegant solutions. "In IT security, I have a feeling that we are making the problem more and more complicated, more and more overloaded with data, and only then do we start to engineer a solution. That will not work."

One-to-one security—one IT person to each hacker or user—is impossible. There is not enough manpower to police the Internet, Prof. Encarnaçáo said, and the world of Internet commerce and youth culture is quickly creating an "anything goes" attitude.

There is a younger generation, Prof. Encarnaçáo noted, for whom "getting information from the Internet is not stealing. There is almost no possibility of getting a lawyer and suing, so it's going to be very, very difficult to find tools to guarantee security. You have to put a lot of effort into guaranteeing that whatever you can do technically you can then follow in the other context."

Programming a Better Mousetrap: OOP

Prof. Max Mühlhäuser, Professor of Computer Science at the University of Darmstadt, suggested that object-oriented programming (OOP) might serve as a good model for designing software and systems that could improve security while complying with the many different privacy policies that exist around the world. Current security solutions, the speaker said, are not up to the tasks they're asked to perform. He pointed to public-key infrastructure (PKI) and firewall technology as falling particularly short of what's needed.

PKI and firewalls are tools made to be used on a daily basis. Unfortunately, thousands of email and Internet providers do not, or don't know how to, implement them in daily applications. While PKI and firewalls are valuable tools, they are often underutilized and misconfigured.

"This means we have not done our homework right," Prof. Mühlhäuser said.

What's needed, he continued, is a "solution that makes humans understand what they are doing and understand the tradeoffs we have in our society between protecting the individual and protecting the society. You protect the individual with privacy protection, you protect the society with ways of revealing things and of proving or falsifying that certain things were going on, or not. This is a tradeoff that society has coped with for centuries, but we do not really know how to handle this in software—especially not in the context of the different balances and different tradeoffs in different countries, under different legislations. We are not aware of how to put this into our globally sold software."

Object orientation might hold the key, however. "Thirty years ago, we understood that our data was in danger because everybody could access it under different software configurations, under maintenance and reuse issues and so on, and we understood that that we should not expose our data to all the software functions that exist. Rather, we saw that it would be helpful to conceal the data and package it with the functions, and that was when we invented object orientation. And if we could come up with a similar model of concealing our data and even functions from a security perspective into individual concealed objects, we could get rid of firewalls in the first place and even get rid of PKI and that might be a road to a solution here."

Evaluating how businesses handle other types of risks helped participants bring the discussion to a more concrete level.

One participant suggested that the latter is true and offered, as an example, some work he had done with BP, the energy and chemicals company. BP, he explained, regularly hires subcontractors to work in its chemical plants, but these people do not necessarily know much about these plants. But sensor networks enable them to identify risky situations and protect both their own lives and the plant itself.

Another participant suggested that certain antifraud measures used by banks might have applicability in security. National Australia Bank, for instance, came up with a way to monitor transactions by its customers and set off triggers when unusual events take place—a particularly large deposit, for example. Likewise, banks have turned to some sophisticated event-monitoring methods to comply with the Basel II accords, which govern how they should manage risk.

The same participant also suggested that traditional techniques for workload management might be of help in security. The same techniques used to identify and shut down runaway queries, for example, might thwart DoS attacks.

These techniques are rarely implemented because they aren't visible until something horrible happens. This, however, is reminiscent of not investing in smoke alarms because "fires are very rare." IT administrators usually put off adding these high-end systems until it's far too late.

Dr. Adam called for more attention to building security into web services. The industry must "make sure that it's starting to work on that from scratch," the speaker said. Likewise, matters of trust will be extremely important with web services. Can an emergency-response agency, for instance, be sure that the lab results or a Geographic Information System (GIS) map it has received are what they purport to be? "Online trust is a major challenge, and I'm not sure that we're doing much work there."

For example, Google Maps is currently facing a censorship issue on a number of fronts, including the blocking out of certain spots in almost every country with strategic political and military targets. Who is to say that the GIS systems purchased or contracted out by governments or individuals aren't similarly crippled?

On the other hand, the ability to zoom in anywhere in the world allows an enemy force to have a similar on-field advantage. When anyone, including a terrorist, can pinpoint a location with astounding accuracy, what are the implications in terms of security and privacy?

Prof. Mühlhäuser continued to point to OOP technologies as a way to visualize and create ontology for security—to create a measurable environment. "We should not expose our data to all the software functions that exist." He suggests concealing the data behind proven and tested security and offering access through OOP techniques. He proposed, in a brave step, that OOP techniques could even do away with firewalls, allowing systems to sit exposed to the network, plugging away at one or two specific tasks, the same idea put forth by virtual participant Bill Cheswick in his discussion of Internet skinny dipping. Strong host security can reduce the need for external security measures.

Going Deeper

Securing networked computers has long been a matter of surrounding them with specialized hardware—such as firewalls—and equipping them with specialized software that tries to detect intruding pieces of code, for instance, and shut them down. Now, researchers are attempting to make the computer itself more self-aware and secure—better able, that is, to recognize malicious code and block its execution. **Justin Rattner,** Director of Intel's Corporate Technology Group, described some intriguing results from research into some new packet-level security techniques.

"I'm a real believer that security starts deep in the system," Mr. Rattner said. "And the platform is fundamentally getting better. It will change significantly over the next several years. We've been doing a couple of things that are very promising, working on virus containment strategies. That's proving to be very robust and very effective."

It's possible, he said, "to completely compromise the operating system. But this has no effect because our technology is embedded in the network interface, below the operating system. It's not signature-based, it's actually based on the packet behavior that has been observed for viruses and worms. They have quite distinct signatures, which in fact is what allows them to propagate so rapidly. For example, many viruses talk amongst themselves in order to "see" which computers they've infected. Even if the inherent code is obfuscated or encrypted, the communication between viral processes is almost always unencrypted.

"The technology we've developed, which we're making available to the community, basically trains on packet behaviors. And it's so good that we essentially had zero escapes. In other words, it doesn't permit any known virus to actually propagate."

Mr. Rattner briefly explained how this technology works: "We contain the virus at the point of infection. We really believe that's the only hope: to contain it at the point of infection and then quickly disconnect that node from the rest of the network. Now, that won't help you in all the other systems connected to the network, but at least going forward we begin to get a handle on things."

Top 5 Up-and-Coming Security Concepts

Biometrics—Forget passwords and PINs. Simply swipe a finger over a tiny scanner and get started. More and more laptops and mobile devices are adding fingerprint readers and the security afforded by these inexpensive devices is quite simple and effective. When investing in a computing fleet, consider adding biometric readers to your systems. Of course, such measures are best used in combination, referred to as two-factor authentication, meaning that even biometrics probably won't do away with passwords.

RFID—Imagine approaching a computer and logging in automatically without touching the keyboard. Although RFID has some privacy concerns, the concept is solid and easily implemented using off-the-shelf equipment. Security through proximity—and maybe a numeric PIN or other innocuous measure—ensures that systems don't remain open when someone goes out to lunch.

"Random" Computing Environments—Windows Vista uses a unique system for "randomizing" its system space. By renaming—and disguising—important files, the OS keeps hackers and viruses at bay. This technology, coupled with on-disk encryption, makes Vista considerably safer than previous Windows incarnations.

Bayesian Filters—Bayesian filters are currently used to identify spam. These filters use a network of information to compare emails to a collection of "common" spam identifiers. By taking this concept further, security programmers can identify odd behaviors and changes that could point to a break-in or threat.

Zero-Day Exploit Teams—When is a security hole the most dangerous? On the day before it's announced publicly. While you might learn about it at 6 a.m. on Monday, rest assured that hackers have been using the exploit to pound your system to bits. Zero-Day Exploit Teams inside an organization can be as big as 50 people or as small as a dedicated security guy inside the IT department. His or her job is simple—keep up to date and patch security holes as soon as they're discovered.

"We're also working very hard to affect the trusted platform and to incorporate devices like TPMs—trusted platform modules—that can store secrets in a secure way. By combining that with certain architectural enhancements, we can provide the capability for secure launch. If the image of a program has been compromised, the machine won't launch it." The machine can determine the state of a program's image by examining its digital signature in a trusted fashion. "That's leading us to this notion of what we call trusted virtual machines," he said, "which really gives us the opportunity, for the first time, to create closed environments on open platforms."

The Final Word

So where are we now? As the forum wound down, participants regrouped around the final answers to creating MAST-compliant devices.

Many security schemes depend on sophisticated cryptographic techniques, but these are often weakened because of lowly software bugs. This problem crops up everywhere. The participants agreed that cryptography is a mathematical field with many complex proofs and little tacit understanding of its concepts and implementation. One cryptographic algorithm gives one kind of security while another gives something entirely different.

Prof. Wolfgang Wahlster, the Director and CEO of DFKI, the German Research Center for Artificial Intelligence, bemoaned this fact, recounting installations at various German banks. "When they have implemented a so-called secure protocol, there turned out to be bugs in the software. We have been asked to verify with our verification tools the software implementation of various security solutions, and we have always found bugs. So, the security of so-called security software is an illusion because there are simple programming bugs in realizing correct security algorithms."

Prof. Wahlster added, "We are very far away from really secure security software." His own organization's study of firewalls found that certain products' software actually contained spyware, evidently put there to surreptitiously feed data to the intelligence agencies of other nations.

"Unbelievable! You buy a firewall, you feel secure, but in the so-called firewall you have intelligence software. I think this is a big problem and really critical. For some security problems, we must get to a level where we can prove that software implementation is really 100 percent guaranteed correct and free of malicious code. In this case, formal program verification is the only way to avoid these massive problems." A nontrivial task, no doubt.

This opens the door for open source security projects. By using open source software, a programming team can implement its own solutions using open source code. By ensuring that everyone in the world will see a particular security solution—and be able to verify its security through peer review—banks and other organizations can ensure that no bugs or holes are overlooked.

Attitude Counts

"We always assume that security is a threat from outside," commented **Tai Chuan Foong,** IM Director for Xian Janssen Pharmaceutical Ltd. "but to me, the threat from inside is even worse. We have PKI, I know it's a pain. We actually spent a lot of money, implemented PKI worldwide, the enterprise directory and everything else. But what we forgot is the training and awareness of our employees."

Mr. Foong went on to describe the one thing in an organization that can't be MAST-compliant: its human beings.

Take, for example, the habits of the average office worker. Printers are often spread out on a large office floor and as documents come out, employees have to trudge over to pick up their documents. These can consist of anything from the office betting pool to confidential plans. When an employee forgets to pick up his documents, what happens? They are thrown into an insecure garbage can behind the building. Build all the security you want, Mr. Foong suggested, but there is always the human factor.

He continued: "My nightmare is phones that have built-in cameras. To me, training and a mindset about intellectual property and protecting information is the key to security, rather than just systems."

"To me, training and a mindset about intellectual property and protecting information is the key to security, rather than just systems."

Prof. Hao Min, Research Director of Auto-ID Labs at Fudan University then had the last word, noting that tight security will depend on hardware and software working in tandem. "In China, we always say 'We have a spear and we have a shield.' You cannot have the best spear that can penetrate everything, and you cannot have a shield that can block everything. What's needed is the right combination of spear and shield, and maybe we can find something like that."

At a high level, two types of security are needed in an enterprise network. The average user wants to make sure nobody is able to get in and extract data and take it. Then the user wants to block any DoS attacks on the network, ensuring that those very pathways that might allow hackers into a system are clear at all times.

To block DoS attacks, users need routers and switches smart enough to understand which packets are bad packets and which ones are good—what's allowed, what's not allowed—and to monitor this process in real time at gigabyte speeds. This is a tall order, but the participants were undaunted.

"Technically, I think we can do it," said Dr. Khosla in a later interview. "However, 90 percent of the infrastructure in the U.S. is owned by private people, and why would any single individual have an interest to upgrade their part of the network when it's not hurting him or her?"

This is why it becomes a very narrow view of security. It's easy for an IT department to say this technical solution exists, but security in the large is a very complex problem that has an interplay of legal, technical and policy issues.

In the end, as Dr. Khosla said, security is a multitechnology problem. People say, "Oh, encryption. Life would be fine if we just encrypted everything." But encryption is not always foolproof—it can be cracked or keys can be lost, rendering encrypted data useless.

Biometrics, perhaps? As we discussed before, the privacy issues are overwhelming for full biometric control. There can be no way to safely create a one-to-one connection between a PC and a human in this way.

Dr. Khosla brought the discussion back to MAST computing: "computing and communication systems that are measurable, available, secure, and trustworthy. And amazingly enough, except for measurable, each one of these properties is nearly *un*obtainable. I don't see how we can create 100 percent secure systems. I don't see how we can create 100 percent trustworthy systems. There are many, many issues that one has to think about."

But is security impossible? Dr. Khosla says no. Using the MAST framework of tradeoffs, security can be implemented onto almost every device. Through techniques like Internet skinny dipping and access control, the problems of security can be turned on their ear. Make systems that react in a measurable way to certain specific stimuli and you've created a secure system. The rest—the contracts, the legislation, and the argument—is just noise.

The True Battle

In the end, the battle for secure systems is a series of tradeoffs. Do I spend millions on a new security system or trust the open source system I have in place? Do I let down my guard and allow a machine to run outside of the firewall? Do I batten down the hatches and risk alienating my customers with onerous security requirements?

IT adversaries have time, money, and a desire to hack a system. IT administrators, on the other hand, are expected to put out fires, maintain systems, and ensure that their users experience acceptable uptime. These goals are incompatible and it's clear that someone will always win, usually to the detriment of the overworked IT guy.

"So take something like the credit card system," said Mr. Cheswick, talking about these tradeoffs. "There is a certain amount of fraud, and the credit card companies know exactly how much of the revenue stream is lost to fraud or at least they have a pretty good idea and when that number gets too big, they tighten up the security and when it is low enough they don't bother. So this is a system where the security is working. It is getting the job done. They are making profits. They are serving customers. People like it and they adjust their efforts as needed to make this work."

It is this give and take—the decision about what is acceptable and what is not in a certain scenario—that allows us to decide where to place our security barriers. No, there is no way to stop all the hackers all of the time. But if we know that the barriers are as secure as we can possibly make them, and that the individual computers inside those barriers also feature robust security, we are headed in the right direction.

Changing the Resolution of Real World Awareness

Excitement continues to mount over the computer's growing awareness of the "real" world. The computer is gaining eyes, ears, a sense of touch, even an odor-sensitive nose, of sorts—the ability, in short, to directly and immediately sense the physical world. Thanks to new networking techniques, improved sensor technologies, and new methods for collecting, filtering, and interpreting floods of "live" data, the computer's real world awareness, or RWA, is vastly more accurate and more useful than ever before.

Early adopters, such as Wal-Mart, Proctor & Gamble, and the U.S. Department of Defense, have shown that the main RWA technology—RFID, or radio-frequency identification—can revolutionize the execution and management of the most challenging business processes. As this chapter will show, RWA's greatest business potential lies in tackling the most complex and difficult business processes, physical processes, mainly, that heretofore have seemed beyond the reach of deep automation because so much costly and error-fraught manual data entry would be involved. Now, however, the means are in hand to automatically collect, at reasonable cost, vast amounts of fresh data about the location, movement, and state of virtually any number and any type of item, of no matter where it's located.

That, as the International Research Forum's lively discussion underscored, means that RWA is poised to rewrite the rules of many businesses. But only, it was emphasized, if enterprises fully appreciate and act on the radical potential of RWA. Simply eliminating the cost and hassle of scanning bar codes—the most obvious reason for considering a move to RFID, for instance—cannot and will not deliver much, if any, ROI. The big payoffs will come from using RWA to rethink the most challenging and daunting physical business processes. RWA should be used to attack chaos and bring to heel problems of such complexity that they would overwhelm current methods.

RWA's potential as a transformative business technology is enhanced by the emergence of new forms of hardware. Physical sensors, constantly shrinking in size, cost, and power requirements, can collect data about everything, from the temperature in a distant food freezer, to the rotational speed of an 18-wheeler's tires, to the frequency and amplitude of tell-tale vibrations in a jet engine flying at 35,000 feet. Down on the ground, all sorts of passive and active RFID tags can wirelessly report the location and movement of virtually any item, from bulk shipping containers, to individual pairs of sneakers, to million-dollar medical machines.

Equally important, RWA is drawing on a new range of powerful data-mining, filtering, and pattern-analysis software designed to find tell-tale relationships in floods of data generated by RFID tags. But challenges remain. In most enterprises, core software applications, such as ERP systems, are not equipped to receive these floods of data, much less make sense of them. As the forum discussion revealed, a fundamental

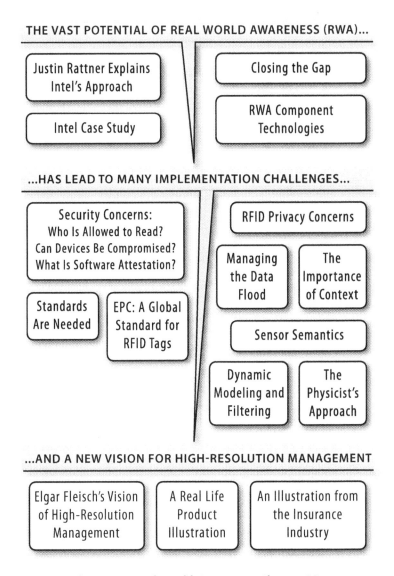

THE VAST POTENTIAL OF REAL WORLD AWARENESS (RWA)...

Justin Rattner Explains Intel's Approach

Closing the Gap

Intel Case Study

RWA Component Technologies

...HAS LEAD TO MANY IMPLEMENTATION CHALLENGES...

Security Concerns:
Who Is Allowed to Read?
Can Devices Be Compromised?
What Is Software Attestation?

RFID Privacy Concerns

Managing the Data Flood

The Importance of Context

Standards Are Needed

EPC: A Global Standard for RFID Tags

Sensor Semantics

Dynamic Modeling and Filtering

The Physicist's Approach

...AND A NEW VISION FOR HIGH-RESOLUTION MANAGEMENT

Elgar Fleisch's Vision of High-Resolution Management

A Real Life Product Illustration

An Illustration from the Insurance Industry

Figure 4-1. Real World Awareness Chapter Map

tension exists between moving to beef up the hub with improved data-handling capabilities and distributing this task to nodes located more or less at the edge of the sensor network. Each approach has its pros and cons, and it will be some time before this tension is fully resolved, most likely with a compromise of some kind.

Closing the Gap

One way of understanding RWA is as the latest, and perhaps last step in a long, continuing story in IT: the steady elimination of so-called media breaks, those physical and logical gaps that exist between IT systems. In the worst cases, to move data across these breaks required a person to read data from one computer's screen and retype it into another's keyboard. This was not only slow but it inevitably introduced errors into the data.

Enterprise resource planning (ERP) systems, typified by SAP's R/3, were an early and important solution to this problem, although only a partial one. They melded into a single set of software, sharing a single database, what before was a collection of disparate and often incompatible IT systems. Later, Ethernet- and Internet-based networks helped to link IT systems within the same company and across enterprise boundaries.

This still left one major information gap, the one that exists between the "real world" entities—their location, velocity, or temperature, for instance—and the models of that world maintained by computers. Bar code scanning has eliminated a great deal of manual data entry, from supermarket checkout lines to rail yards, but networks of RFID and physical sensors promise to close the gap even further.

Promises and Challenges

Reviewing and then building on the forum discussion, this chapter looks at some of the more important factors and challenges, both social and technical, that are shaping the conceptualization and practical use of RWA. Among them are: the public's concern for privacy; the need for better standards; and the call for improved methods of storing, analyzing, and acting on floods of fine-grained data.

The most obvious advantage of using sensors to collect data in real time is simply a reduction in the manual entering of information, an activity that's notorious for introducing errors into enterprise data. By eliminating the so-called media break (see "Closing the Gap"), RWA technologies can ensure that IT systems have cleaner, more accurate data to work with. Tedium is reduced, mistakes eliminated, thoroughness all but guaranteed, and effectiveness enhanced.

Eliminating media breaks is such a big step forward that it can easily overshadow RWA's other benefits. By supplying not only cleaner but more and much fresher data at low cost, RWA can yield unprecedented views into important physical processes like multi-tier supply chains, flows of raw materials, and work-in-progress within factories. This high-resolution view, to use the elegant term coined by one of the forum's participants, is making possible highly competitive, industry-changing business processes and business models, even in nonmanufacturing industries such as car insurance.

Intel's Success with RWA

Justin Rattner, Intel Senior Fellow, opened the forum's RWA session by describing the chip giant's experiences with the technology.

He explained that on Intel's wafer fabrication lines, the rooms full of equipment where it actually makes microchips, round silicon wafers full of chips-in-progress often get misplaced. Workers often simply park a stack of wafers somewhere, mid-processing, and forget them. The wafer holders may have tags with notes written on them, but still, many of them end up getting scrapped, Mr. Rattner said.

But now, he said, by using RFID tags to track these wafers electronically, Intel has eliminated this waste, increased the effective yields of its fabrication lines, cut costs, and achieved a greater understanding of its entire fabrication process.

RWA technology, Mr. Rattner went on, will have profound effects on everyday life. He pointed to the Grand Challenge Car Race, sponsored by the U.S. Defense Advanced Research Projects Agency (DARPA) and held in the fall of 2005. It saw 23 driverless, self-guided vehicles try to make their way, unaided, across 132 miles of desert terrain southwest of Las Vegas. Just four cars managed to finish, with Stanford University's car, called Stanley, winning the $2 million grand prize.

"That is a real world example of a complete sensor-affector system. Those vehicles had to deal with a completely natural environment. There was no human documentation, no human assistance whatsoever,"

Justin Rattner is an Intel Senior Fellow and Director of Intel's Corporate Technology Group. He also serves as the corporation's Chief Technology Officer (CTO). He heads Intel's microprocessor, communications, and systems technology labs and Intel Research. In 1989, Mr. Rattner was named Scientist of the Year by R&D Magazine for his leadership in parallel and distributed computer architecture. In December 1996, ABC World News featured Mr. Rattner as Person of the Week for his visionary work on the Department of Energy ASCI Red System, the first computer to sustain one trillion operations per second (one teraflops) and the fastest computer in the world between 1996 and 2000. In 1997, Mr. Rattner was honored as one of the *Computing 200* individuals with the greatest impact on the U.S. computer industry today, and was subsequently profiled in the book *Wizards and Their Wonders* from ACM Press.

Mr. Rattner has received two Intel Achievement Awards for his work in high-performance computing and advanced cluster communication architecture. He is a longstanding member of Intel's Research Council and Academic Advisory Council. He currently serves as the Intel executive sponsor for Cornell University, where he serves on the External Advisory Board for the School of Engineering. Mr. Rattner joined Intel in 1973. He was named its first Principal Engineer in 1979 and the fourth Intel Fellow in 1988. Prior to joining Intel, he held positions with Hewlett-Packard Company and Xerox Corporation. He received bachelor's and master's degrees from Cornell University in Electrical Engineering and Computer Science in 1970 and 1972, respectively.

Mr. Rattner said. His conclusion: The day will come when car makers like BMW and Mercedes produce cars that take over when a driver begins to nod out at the wheel. "It won't be next year or maybe even in the next five years, but I wouldn't put it 20 or 30 years in the future," Mr. Rattner said. "If you take real world awareness to its limit, you can imagine systems of just that sort."

RWA's Component Technologies
Intel Senior Fellow Justin Rattner sees RWA technologies falling into the following categories:

- Physical positioning, or location-sensing schemes, which use GPS signals from space or that triangulate on signals from wireless local area network (LAN) access points or cellular base stations
- Biometrics, for identifying the unique physical characteristics of individuals
- Physical sensors, which can measure temperatures, capture images through machine vision, recognize sounds and odors, and measure other physical parameters
- Wireless technologies for connecting to sensors inexpensively and flexibly. These include ultra-wideband (UWB), WiMax, and self-organizing mesh networks.
- Back-end systems for collecting and analyzing floods of data pouring in from far-flung networks of sensors
- Analysis techniques, such as machine learning and statistical computing, which can help mine volumes of sensor data and identify meaningful events and patterns.

Mr. Rattner concluded by noting that progress in RWA will be tempered by a number of technical issues, perhaps the most important of which is the "torrent of data" that large-scale sensor networks will inevitably create. He said Intel is looking seriously at ways of putting more computing power and analytic intelligence out at the edge of these nets as a way to filter and reduce the influx of raw data. That will likely require innovation in architectures for distributed computing, which Intel and several startup companies are working on. The alternative is to bring the sensor data, in raw untouched form, to a central hub—an ERP system, most likely—and analyze it there. The hub approach will require innovation, too, because ERP systems aren't currently set up to handle the volumes of data that will be involved. As in the Web 2.0 discussion, where social-media technologies such as wikis and blogs coexist with transactional ERP systems, the question of edge versus hub is critical to RWA.

Case Study: Intel

Mr. Rattner reported that Intel has enjoyed "extraordinary success" in applying certain advanced statistical techniques to RWA data collected in its factories:

"We have had quite a bit of first-hand experience at Intel, again, largely in experimental settings, using the sensor technologies in our high-volume manufacturing processes," he said. "Using statistical techniques, we've been able to pinpoint a troublesome piece of equipment in the wafer fab[rication]. The machine was actually in spec, operating within its [proper] range, but it was at the high end of that range and that was resulting in significant loss at the end of the fab. Were it not for our substantial collection of data throughout the fab and then the deep analysis of that data, we would have never understood the real loss at the end."

This case study was referred to later in the discussion. The larger topic was how and where to analyze sensor data. Spy agencies that analyze satellite images, noted Michael Schrage of MIT, typically have to know what they are looking for in order to find it. Yet the example of Intel gaining a better understanding of its chip fabrication line appears to be the opposite.

"Even though Intel's machine was performing within spec," the company was having yield problems, Mr. Schrage pointed out. "You do not necessarily know, *ex-ante*, what information you wish to collect. You can make a completely logical decision and focus on exceptions, and yet, never catch the machine that was causing the problem because you have made a rule that says, 'I am only going to look for the exceptions'."

Had Intel pushed the decision-making out to the edge and made its machine entirely self-diagnosing, Mr. Schrage said, it never would have discovered where the problem existed. The machine would have reported that it was performing within preset parameters and no trouble would have been indicated.

Security Concerns

While the idea of computers sensing the world engenders excitement or fear, depending on your perspective, questions related to security are asked much less frequently. Who is allowed to read RWA data? How can one be sure that it has not been tampered with? **Dr. Pradeep Khosla** of Carnegie-Mellon University explained the security problem that arises with increased dependence on sensor networks and what might be done about it.

"There is a very big security issue with sensor networks, even if you just limit yourself to RFID," Dr. Khosla said. RFID tags of the kind that Wal-Mart and other retailers are beginning to use have little if any security attached to them. "I can read a passive or an active RFID [tag] without any problem, even when I have no right to access it." In theory, he explained, someone from a retailer could surreptitiously enter a competitor's store and use a portable RFID reader to learn about the inventory on shelves and perhaps in the back room, too.

"There is a very big security issue with sensor networks."

But that's only the tip of the proverbial iceberg, Dr. Khosla said. Sensors will be attached to critical infrastructure such as roadways, waterways, dams, lakes, water supplies, power systems, power plants, nuclear plants, and oil pipelines, but without special measures, they will be vulnerable to attack. It might well be possible for an adversary to reprogram sensors so that they would send false information about the health of a remote facility. "Unless there is a way for you to figure out that he reprogrammed it or hacked into the network to which it's connected," Dr. Khosla said, "you could unknowingly receive information from it that is all garbage. And then, you'd be making decisions based on that [bad] information."

There's also the potential of executing a DoS attack on sensor nodes by repeatedly pinging them, making them respond again and again, and thereby draining them of battery power.

Software Attestation

Dr. Khosla's research focuses on software attestation, or being able to prove that software in a remote sensor has not been meddled with. "Is that node running the code that I put on it, or is it different?" he asked. "Just getting a simple yes or no for an answer is a big deal." Methods have been developed to mathematically prove the integrity of any particular piece of code. They call for calculating a mathematical hash of the code and comparing it to a similar hash generated at a known point in time. If the two hashes match up, the code is intact.

However, this approach is susceptible to attacks. An attacker could insert a single line of code that would intercept the request for a new hash and send the approved hash function back as its answer.

Dr. Khosla said he and fellow researchers have come up with an alternative method. Instead of hashing the sensor's entire memory contents at once, their software traverses the sensor's memory at random. "We might have you pose 100 queries," he explained. "Mathematically, one can show that if you do this a reasonable number of times, the probability of traversing the whole memory is close to one. But an attacker could never know how that random traversal is going to happen. So, we use multiple small hashes to create the whole hash. But the attacker would never know."

Dr. Khosla is also working on ways of authenticating sensor data, a challenge given the computational intensity of encryption algorithms and the limited battery life available in sensors. A colleague, Adrian Perrig, has come up with novel, time-based algorithms that execute in about one-hundredth of the time of normal encryption algorithms but yield the same encryption strength.

The Public Response to RFID

Prof. Dr. Wolfgang Wahlster, Director and CEO of DFKI, the German Research Center for Artificial Intelligence and Professor of Computer Science at Saarland University, addressed the public perceptions of RFID. While RFID's benefits to suppliers and retailers receives much attention, Prof. Wahlster said, the man in the street is generally ignored. "The consumer is not very interested in 'master logistic supply chain management' but instead, feels he loses his privacy [to RFID systems]," Prof. Wahlster said. "We must exploit this technology for the customer's sake, too."

"We must exploit this technology for the customer's sake, too."

Prof. Wahlster pointed to the Cyberstore of DFKI, in Saarbrücken, Germany as an operation that shows the public what's to be gained from RWA. DFKI's Cyberstore uses these technologies to create what it calls "mixed reality shopping." As shoppers push their carts through the store, their location is automatically monitored and RFID tags on items in their carts are monitored, too. This enables a screen on the cart to present comparison-shopping information along with suggestions about additional products they might purchase, such as accessories for the items already in their carts. In-shop navigation is provided by DFKI's intelligent shopping assistant together with proactive product information. In addition, cellular handsets and digital cameras are programmed to explain their own features to anyone who picks them up, Prof. Wahlster explained.

He added that RFID tag technologies are advancing and broadening their range of application. Tickets for the then-upcoming World Cup football tournament contained RFID tags as a way to prevent counterfeiting. Research labs are creating polymer-based tags that can be sewn into clothing items and even washed without losing their data.

"When we introduce this technology," he urged, "we want to avoid protests from normal citizens." When clothing makers added smart labels to their wares, protests and boycotts broke out at certain stores. Anti-RFID protests flared up in Germany and elsewhere. "The only way to fight this is to show people that the technology brings them important advantages, too," Prof. Wahlster said.

Privacy and RFID

The issue of RFID as a potential and perceived threat to privacy also came up for discussion. Asked Prof. Hao Min: "How can we have an infrastructure where I would be able to specify what, where, and when data could be linked to my identity?" He noted that authorities in Singapore used RFID to track individuals as a way to help contain an outbreak of the SARS virus. And to this day, "privacy is still an issue" for people who lived through that episode.

Another participant pointed out that RWA isn't solely RFID and that "smart items," costing more than RFID tags, will become quite

"That is the challenge for us, to really think about how we can explain RWA to lay audiences who are skeptical and perhaps even afraid of RWA technology."

important in people's lives. "Maybe we should emphasize that we are talking about more sophisticated solutions, costing not pennies but Euros10. They will provide a service and bring value to the masses by accomplishing all sorts of interesting things. That is the challenge for us, to really think about how we can explain RWA to lay audiences who are skeptical and perhaps even afraid of RWA technology."

In fact, it might be useful to show the public audience that a continuum exists that stretches from RWA's smart items to the embedded computing systems—found in cars, home entertainment systems, and kitchen appliances, for instance—with which most people are quite familiar and comfortable.

Standards Needed—Apply Within

As in every other area of computing, standards will be absolutely critical to RWA's success. By definition, RWA calls for the movement of data between disparate systems. Without some agreement on how this data is to be coded, formatted, and given context, individual pieces of RWA data will inevitably lose meaning as they're transferred from one system to another. Considering that different brands of gear may be used on the same sensor network and that partners up and down a complex supply chain will each run their own IT systems and use their own information schemas, the need for standards is overwhelming.

The good news is that bodies like ISO and EPCglobal Inc. have published a fair number of standards and are working full speed ahead on additional ones. One of the most important of those already published is the EPC Information Service (EPCIS), which specifies the formatting of data used to identify and describe individual objects, and events that involve those objects, so that trading partners can share the data across their different systems.

RFID Privacy Concerns

The advent of RFID technology has prompted many activists to raise the alarm about its potential for intruding on people's privacy. One of the most vocal groups is **Consumers Against Supermarket Privacy Invasion and Numbering (Caspian).** Some of these groups' concerns are legitimate while others appear to be misinformed paranoia. Clearly, RFID tags enable a finer-grained tracking of products and buying habits within stores, beyond what's already being done extensively with supermarket checkout cards, for instance. It seems doubtful, however, that consumer goods makers would surreptitiously install tag readers in public spaces or, even more unlikely, in consumers' homes. Still, that's exactly what some activists say they are afraid of—a world in which there's no escape from the prying gaze of RFID readers. Perceived threats include:

- Consumers' shopping habits will be monitored to a new level within stores
- Consumers' physical movements will be traceable in the streets and other public spaces
- Usage of individual products will be monitored in homes with "smart" refrigerators and tag readers in home doorways
- Tagged medicine bottles will monitor people's drug usage
- Tagged currency will enable the monitoring of spending habits
- Smart bank cards may be scanned in wallets as shoppers enter stores, thereby tipping merchants to which people should be treated to more personal service than others

Managing the Data Flood

The discussion now opened up to all participants, and they turned first to the problem of where to process, or analyze, the volumes of data that will be generated by large networks of sensors—out at the edge of those networks or at their centers, or hubs. This is a fundamental tension shaping the planning for large-scale RFID deployments.

SAP's **Prof. Lutz Heuser** said that masses of data should not even hit the network. "It should be already processed, at least somewhat, before it hits the network. The challenge is this: With thousands and tens of hundreds of thousands of data sources, is the network capable

EPC: A Global Standard for RFID Tags

To be successful, RFID technology will require the creation of many new technical standards. Leading the way in this process is EPCglobal Inc., a not-for-profit organization headquartered in Brussels. As of December 2006, 1,000 companies worldwide had signed up to use EPCglobal's standards. These companies range from consumer packaged goods to life sciences to footwear to logistics.

The primary EPCglobal standard is the electronic product code, or EPC. It defines exactly how companies should build numeric codes that would uniquely identify their products. These codes would actually be programmed into RFID tags, replacing or augmenting the traditional printed bar code. Each EPC code consists of several data fields that identify the manufacturer of a product as well as the product itself, a size 14 Air Jordan sneaker made by Nike, for instance. At a length of 96 bits, the EPC standard can uniquely identify 268 million companies, each with 16 million product classes, and 68 billion serial numbers in each of those classes—enough, in other words, to cover all products manufactured around the world for many years to come.

EPCglobal is working on many other RFID standards. It has proposed certain radio frequencies for ID tags to use, and it is helping to define how an Object Name Service (ONS) might work. Like the Internet's domain name system (DNS), the ONS would match any item's EPC tag number to the address of a specific server that contained information about the item—a facility that's key to helping enterprises make use of RFID data.

To help different applications, perhaps running within different enterprises, to share RFID data, EPC has come up with a standard called ALE, which stands for application-level event. Much as SQL enables disparate applications to share a database by hiding its low-level details, so does ALE shield applications from the details of sensor networks and the volumes of low-level data they generate.

of dealing with that data?" Maybe it is actually necessary, he noted, for reasons of legal proof, warranty, or liability, to maintain a central store of all the original sensor data. But the more data that can be kept off the network, the better.

Dr. Maria Orlowska, Professor of Information Systems at the University of Queensland, wondered aloud if it's actually possible to make sufficient sense of floods of RWA data by scanning it merely once, on the fly, as is done with so-called stream-processing algorithms. These techniques, which are currently being extensively studied by many research groups and some of which are even being commercialized, look for relationships between the values in selected data entries immediately as the data is generated and may trigger alerts when certain patterns are spotted. This type of technology is definitely useful, for example in financial applications deployed at a stock exchange, where floods of live market data must be analyzed on the fly for the sake of any number of different trading strategies. But is on-the-fly analysis really a way of dealing with all sensor-generated data?

"Very few applications are built exclusively on associative computations," Dr. Orlowska said. "One must consider under what conditions you can draw conclusions from a stream of data, regardless of how much data your application consumed. When you add another data item to the analyzed stream, you must know how to modify the current result." There are problems with analyzing a single scan of data, which is in effect what happens when sensor data is simply read into main memory: "In general, data mining," she added, "cannot be performed accurately with a single data scan in main memory." The data must be stored first because a single scan of data in memory "cannot achieve the accuracy that is possible with multiple data scans, which the fastest and most precise algorithms do." The problem is not the capacity of main memory, either, as Dr. Orlowska clarifies: "This is not a limitation of computers but of the nature of calculations to be performed. In most cases, the data must be stored for further consumption and analysis by more sophisticated applications."

Alexander Schill, Professor of Computer Networks at Dresden University of Technology, built on that thought. "We are talking about the challenges of creating very complex context services and the measurements that we have heard about, temperature, location, and so on, are only a starting point. These are much too low-level for many applications. We have to think about

"We are talking about the challenges of creating very complex context services..."

higher-level abstractions, which come with uncertainties. You may have a certain location, but concerning the overall environmental descriptions, you have to tackle uncertainties."

Sensor Semantics

Sensor data can be aggregated and analyzed on the spot, suggested **Dr. Ike Nassi,** Senior Vice President at SAP Research, Americas. He offered the example of the modern automobile, which has as many as 70 sensors. Data collected by some set of these may be interpreted as indicating that a car is in danger of aquaplaning on a wet highway and losing control. It may be possible to transmit this observation wirelessly to nearby cars, warning them of the danger. The question is, how can this sense of danger be conveyed? He reported that a project involving Mercedes and BMW came up with a "risk ontology," which described a variety of states a car could be in—not at the sensor level, but at a higher level. "This is distributed computing, transmitting only interesting information—for example, the fact that there is aquaplaning taking place—because all the low-level, sensor detail is not interesting for another car."

Filtering Data

Filtering data, managing events, and handling exceptions struck the forum participants as areas particularly ripe for further exploration.

Dr. Peter Kürpick, member of the executive board of Software AG, wondered whether or not it's always necessary to capture and store masses of low-level detail or only significant exceptions. "If we are talking about terabytes of data, do we want to store all of them just to find out six months later that this RFID tag on this package at that point in time had that measurement? I don't know whether that is of much interest. If we are fishing for events, if we are looking for specific events, then look at how physicists do this. They are filtering data at the edges right away, at the moment that an event happens" (see "The Physicists' Approach").

Harking back to the earlier discussion of Semantic Web issues, Dr. Kürpick said that RFID might be an area where data and semantics are coupled. "If an RFID chip or some sensor measures the temperature, it

---

The Importance of Context

Prof. Alexander Schill spoke at the forum about the pressing need for global and distributed context services.

A context service would make it easier for trading partners to interpret each other's RFID data. Imagine an RFID tag moving by a tag reader at a distribution center. The tag itself contains only a unique ID number, but the context service might provide associated data such as where that pallet had come from, where it is intended to go, a description of its contents, and when it was manufactured—all items that would be helpful to different parties in the supply chain. Like URLs that point to particular servers and files on the Web, the context service would enable unique tag ID numbers to serve as pointers to rich database entries in far-flung servers. EPCglobal has proposed a standard for such content services.

According to Prof. Schill, "We are quite far away from that. It would be very hard to negotiate any appropriate level for such a standard. We started many years ago with things like RDF, resource description framework, an XML-based metadata model, and already, several years on, this is leading absolutely nowhere. It is much too low level an abstraction. There were many extensions to RDF, but I think we are far away from a workable, global context service."

---

is not going to measure anything but the temperature. So, if you have a good way of defining that, that it is really temperature that matters and nothing else, you introduce a level of semantics to the whole game of data and information. It could be temperature, it could be order, it could be chemicals, or vibration, or anything."

Dr. Kürpick also noted that the example of a car signaling others about its own aquaplaning troubles is not as straightforward as it might seem. Just because one kind of car is having such trouble doesn't necessarily mean that all cars, each with its own physics, so to speak, are in equal danger. Indeed, broadcasting such a warning might actually lead to massive congestion as many cars respond to it by needlessly slowing down.

"The semantic level does make a difference," he said, "because to simply make the assumption that all cars are going to respond comparably may be a perverse simplification. A just-in-time design of filters may be the real issue that arises with greater volumes of data. How do you quickly design filters and mechanisms that are statistically significant, that align to the business issues that you identify?"

At this point, the formal forum discussion of RWA came to an end. The participants had identified many of the challenges facing the industry and customers as they try to make use of the RWA concept: the tensions between processing data at the edge versus the hub of networks; the need for educating the public about the benefits of RWA, and RFID in particular, while also enhancing the technology's security and privacy; and the need to hammer out standards in the areas of data formats and semantics.

The High-Resolution Management Vision of Prof. Fleisch

In time, all of these problems will be addressed. But those with a clear vision of how to use RWA needn't wait to make important and valuable progress. That's the message of one forum contributor, **Prof. Elgar Fleisch,** Co-Chair of the Auto-ID Labs and Professor of Technology Management at ETH Zurich and University of St. Gallen, in Switzerland.

In a later interview, Prof. Fleisch expanded on his comments at the forum, emphasizing the importance of understanding RWA's full impact and describing his vision of how the technology can support entirely new business models that may give innovative companies strong competitive advantages.

Misunderstanding of RWA is widespread, Prof. Fleisch began. "When people talk about real world awareness, they often think of it as merely a replacement for bar codes. But if you think along that line, limiting your vision to merely replacing one technology with another, real world awareness will never work." Eliminating media breaks, while crucial, is actually only the first step of using RWA to its fullest.

It's critical, said Prof. Fleisch, to grasp the full potential of RWA as a transformative technology, one that can provide an entirely new basis for managing physical processes. And by using that basis properly, he argued, corporations can gain competitive advantage. RWA can support brand-new ways of managing existing as well as new business processes; innovative services, products, and business models; and major improvements in managing relationships between suppliers and customers.

This still leaves one major media break to do away with, Prof. Fleisch said, specifically the one that exists between the "real world and the data we have in our system. We still need human beings to key in that data, and if we don't key it in then we have bar code scanners, but we still scan the data in mostly by hand. That's expensive, error-prone, and takes lots of time."

"Now imagine a world where the marginal cost of getting data about what's actually going on in the real world is close to zero."

"Now," he posited, "imagine a world where the marginal cost of getting data about what's actually going on in the real world is close to zero. That would not only change the cost of data acquisition; it would have a rebound effect because leverage is very strong. It would make you scan the real world way, way more often."

Of Blind Spots and Hi-Res Management

Prof. Fleisch used a visual metaphor to explain the advantages to be gained from collecting so much fresh data. More data amounts to a higher-resolution image of the process or activity that is producing this data. "You can only manage what you can measure," he said. "But now, because you are able to see more, you can measure more and manage with greater detail." RWA, he said, is nothing less than a very powerful new measuring tool for management.

And new measuring instruments, he pointed out, have the power to "radically change" a discipline. He pointed to the ways X-ray and MRI technologies have given medical professionals a way to peer inside the living organism and learn more about how it works. That, in turn, has yielded new ways to heal. Likewise, microscopes changed how biology was studied, and other measuring instruments revolutionized physics.

The Physicists' Approach

Any IT manager cringing at potential floods of RFID data should consider what physicists will be coping with in their search for the elusive Higgs boson, an exceedingly short-lived and possibly nonexistent subatomic particle.

At CERN, the high-energy physics lab in Geneva, Switzerland, the hunt for Higgs bosons will produce 40 terabytes (TB) of data *per second!* But thanks to some homegrown filtering techniques, that flood will be quickly reduced to a reasonable 100 megabytes per second.

The search for Higgs will start with CERN's Large Hadron Collider—an accelerator slated to begin operating in 2007—sending two clouds of protons hurtling at nearly the speed of light, in opposite directions from each other, around a 27-km underground ring of superconducting magnets. Although these two clouds will cross paths 40 million times every second, the clouds will pass through each other virtually unscathed. On average, only 20 actual proton collisions will occur with each passing of the two clouds. And according to theory, the chance that one of these collisions will produce a Higgs particle is a mind-numbingly small 1 in 1,015.

Of course, when there is a collision, and two protons burst apart in a curlicue spray of subatomic particles, CERN's researchers will be prepared to catch all the action. A cylindrical array of 100 million detectors will keep the collision zone fully covered, ready to record detailed images of each newly created particle's trajectory. (In fact, if a Higgs boson is created, theory predicts that it will very quickly split into still more subparticles, and physicists actually will be hoping to see signs of those remnants.)

It's these particle detectors that will produce the 40TB of raw data, but within a few microseconds, this volume will be reduced by a factor of 400, and then again by another 10 to 100 times. Two CERN-designed grids of nearly 1,000 PC servers, running in parallel over an ultra-high-speed interconnect, will immediately identify the few regions of images that may warrant further investigation and discard the rest.

Still, each year of running this experiment is expected to saddle CERN researchers with 1,000TB more image data to pore through. Given that the search for the Higgs boson will likely last a decade or more, the resulting 10,000TB database will be far larger than anything in use by commercial enterprises. Stored on tape, a 100TB subset of this imagery could take nearly a month to scan just once. With hundreds of investigators each wishing to run their own analyses, that pace is untenable.

(continued on next page)

(continued from previous page)
Falling prices for hard-disk arrays will surely help, but CERN's IT research-ers are also working on ways of speeding the search process by creating periodic summaries of their data.

As the birthplace of the World Wide Web, CERN is certainly a place to watch for leading-edge ideas in IT. So who knows, even if the Higgs particle turns out to be mythical, the high-volume data-filtering tech-niques it inspired may one day help enterprises plow through their own mountains of RFID data.

Now, RWA can help people to scan the physical world of things that are moving and interacting with other things. "Real world aware-ness will generate high-resolution data at no cost, and that will help us to understand how the world really works," he said.

In Prof. Fleisch's view, this new understand-ing will help not only with fine-tuning existing business processes but, more importantly, it will spur the creation of entirely new processes, new businesses, and new business models.

"Real world awareness will generate high-resolution data at negligible cost, and that will help us to understand how the world really works."

Seek Improvement in Complexity

Not all organizations will be able to profitably make use of RWA data, Prof. Fleisch warned. "If you have a simple problem to solve, if you have a simple process and you don't need high-resolution data, you don't need RFID." If a doctor sees that a patient has only a small cut, there's no need for an X-ray. But a supply chain that's frequently making mistakes is likely to benefit from the use of high-resolution data. The reason for those mistakes, he explained, is usually that the logic in the relevant IT systems is not of sufficient complexity. Complex processes cannot be managed with simple rules. "Try to translate Shakespeare with a vocabulary of 100 words in the target language. It won't work. The only way to manage very complex things is to add complexity to the management system, and that is precisely what high-resolution management is really doing in a very smart way."

 **Elgar Fleisch** is Professor of Information Management at the Department of Management, Technology, and Economics at ETH Zürich. He is also Professor for Technology Management and Director of the Institute of Technology Management at the University of St. Gallen (ITEM-HSG). After graduating from the Institution of Higher Technical Education in Engineering, Austria, Professor Fleisch, an Austrian citizen, studied business administration and computer science at the University of Vienna and wrote his Ph.D. thesis at the Vienna University of Economics and Business Administration and the Institute for Advanced Studies in the area of artificial intelligence in production scheduling. In 1994, Professor Fleisch started his work at the University of St. Gallen. From 1996 to 1997, he founded and served IMG Americas Inc. in Philadelphia, as its CEO. In 2000, he was accepted as assistant professor at the University of St. Gallen.

Today, Professor Fleisch conducts research on information management issues in the ubiquitously networked world, including the dynamics of information systems in conjunction with business processes and real-world problems. Together with Prof. Friedemann Mattern of the Institute of Pervasive Computing at ETH Zürich, he leads the M-Lab and cochairs the Auto-ID Labs, which specify the infrastructure for the "Internet of Things." Professor Fleisch is also a cofounder of Intellion AG and a member of several steering committees in research, education, and industry.

Retail Promotions

To illustrate his approach, Prof. Fleisch described an episode in which a U.S. consumer goods manufacturer wished to promote its products at a large retail chain. Father's Day was approaching, and the manufacturer, seeing an opportunity to promote its products as gifts, wanted to get its promotional materials onto the sales floors of as many of the retailer's stores as possible, exactly one week before Father's Day itself. Well before this deadline, the manufacturer prepared its materials and shipped them to thousands of the retailer's stores.

Now, how could the manufacturer find out how many store managers actually put this material on display in time for the big day? It would

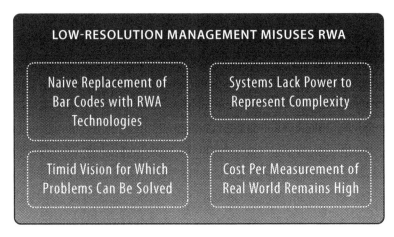

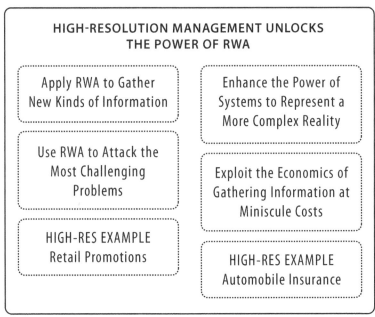

Figure 4-2. High-resolution management unlocks the power of RWA

cost too much to inspect more than a few stores in person. The solution: the manufacturer added RFID tags to the promotional materials
that would register when each store received the promotional displays
and put them on its floor.

The findings turned out to be quite surprising. About 50 percent of the
stores put up the displays well before the assigned day and without any

advertising tie-in to encourage customers to make purchases. Another 20 percent of the stores displayed the materials *after* Father's Day was over. Finally, it was discovered that in a control group, where the timing was done correctly, sales of the manufacturer's products actually rose by 20 percent—a remarkable gain for any retailing promotion.

"If you don't measure, you can't manage. And if you can't manage, then your error rate will be very high."

According to Prof. Fleisch, this episode illustrates a very simple concept: "If you don't measure, you can't manage. And if you can't manage, then your error rate will be very high." Prof. Fleisch, who consulted with the manufacturer on this experiment, recalled its managers assuring him that "there is no problem" with the timing of promotions. "Why did they think there was no problem?" he asked. "Because they couldn't see, because they couldn't measure it."

If everybody has a low-resolution view, he noted, then everything seems fine because everybody makes the same mistakes. But if some companies start to view the world at a higher resolution than others, they will be able to gain a competitive advantage. Examples of this abound, he said, in everything from managing promotions, to keeping retail shelves stocked, to understanding customers, to managing production activities.

"Every company has its blind spots," the professor noted. "And like our brain, which gets used to our eye's blind spot, companies don't see where they have big problems because they have grown accustomed to not seeing those problems. But once they start measuring down to the individual store and product, for instance, their blind spots become quite apparent."

The stock-out problem in retailing—customers discovering that an item they came to buy isn't on the shelf, which prompts them to buy a competitor's product or leave for another store—is another common challenge that high-resolution data can help to alleviate. Retailers, said Prof. Fleisch, say, "We have checkout data—we have everything." In fact, they typically consult their checkout data once a day, and that's usually at the end of the day. It's not economical to constantly send employees down the aisles to check for empty shelves. So, companies usually convince themselves that they don't have stock-out problems. But if they'd start measuring, Prof. Fleisch said, they'd find that on average, 7 percent of all products do have a stock-out problem.

Reinventing Car Insurance

How can RWA support highly competitive new business models and service concepts? Prof. Fleisch used Progressive Insurance and UNIQA Insurance, as a great example of how RWA can shake up a fairly staid industry. No, he explained, Progressive is not sticking RFID tags on anything or anyone. It has, though, tested the idea of using GPS receivers to bring down the cost of auto insurance. (UNIQA is taking a similar though not identical approach.)

In effect, Progressive has created a "pay as you drive" insurance plan in which each customer's monthly payments are tied to his or her actual driving habits. (The company has since licensed its scheme to Norwich Union, a U.K. insurer, which has been actively marketing it.) First, customers agree to have a "black box" installed in their car—a GPS receiver that tracks the car's movements and periodically sends this information to their insurer. By correlating this information with other sets of data, the insurance company can now map the car's minute-

"The high-resolution view enables Progressive to better see the risk it is working with and change its relationship to customers accordingly, to rewrite insurance contracts one by one."

by-minute travels and determine how much risk the driver has incurred. Depending on what distances the car has gone, the kinds of neighborhoods it may have visited, the times of day or night it was on the road, its maximum speeds, the weather conditions, and even if the driver used a cell phone while driving, the car owner's monthly premium can be recalculated to reflect actual risk.

Prof. Fleisch said that young women, especially, have been found to appreciate the new insurance plan because it gives them a better price than they might have to pay elsewhere. They don't have to shoulder the burden of high-risk young males—the bane of all car insurers because of their statistically high accident rate. "The high-resolution view enables Progressive to better see the risk it is working with and change its relationship to customers accordingly, to rewrite insurance contracts one by one."

The payoff for the insurer is striking. Because it can safely charge low-risk drivers a lower-than-usual monthly premium, the GPS-equipped insurer tends to attract more than its share of exactly that kind of driver. Likewise, higher-risk drivers tend to seek their insurance elsewhere. As a result, the insurer ends up managing much less risk than traditional competitors.

In fact, the insurer can actually use its remote monitoring to win young males' business, as well. If a 20-year-old agrees not to drive weekend evenings and nights, when most of the worst car accidents happen, he can lower his premium considerably. Of course, if he does drive during the high-risk period, the GPS recorder in his car would report that infraction and his premium would be raised. Knowing this, he will likely think twice and call for a taxi, instead. Thus, in Britain at least, where car insurance is particularly expensive, insurance has the power to actually change behavior.

Prof. Fleisch reemphasized that it's not enough to think of RWA, and especially RFID, as merely a low-cost replacement for bar codes. That replacement will certainly save companies some money, he said, but savings will be ridiculously low compared to the investment they'd have to make.

Prof. Fleisch forgives companies for missing the true potential of RWA. "The fact is, most of the problems you can solve with RWA are problems that managers are not yet aware of in any detail. They might know their stores have stock-out situations, or that they're experiencing theft or counterfeit products, but since those problems are so costly to measure, they don't get measured. And therefore, they don't get managed effectively, either."

Prof. Fleisch's advice to newcomers is to "bring in an expert to help guide you" through what he called the second- and third-level thinking of RWA. And above all, don't be afraid of thinking big, very big. "Don't go for simple problems. Go for areas where you think there's chaos. Go for complex scenarios. Go for problems that today look unmanageable." It's there, he maintains, that RWA will truly shine and pay for itself many times over.

IT as a Tool for Growth and Development

5

Globalization and its attendant trends—democratization, development, interdependence, and others—can prove a force for immense good if they are properly harnessed. However, to date, the record of the world community in achieving this goal is mixed, at best; if it does not improve, a number of threats and risks, from terrorism to environmental degradation to expanding human misery, are likely to emerge.

— "Global Policymaking for Information and Communications Technologies," Implementation Team on Global Policy Participation, G8 Digital Opportunity Task Force, 2002, p. 11

In *The World Is Flat*, the *New York Times* columnist Thomas Friedman argues that we have entered the era of "Globalization 3.0," an era in which nations, corporations, and now individuals compete for opportunities on a global scale. (The title of his book has become a shorthand signifier for all of globalization's successes thus far—the creation of economic opportunities and even wealth in the developing world through the relocation of global chains to India, China, and beyond.) Friedman is very clear that "the lever that is enabling individuals and groups to go global so easily and so seamlessly is not horsepower, and not hardware, but software—all sorts of new applications—in conjunction with the creation of a global fiber-optic network that has made us all next-door neighbors."

Throughout his book, Friedman wholeheartedly credits the evolution of information and communication technologies (ICT) as the driver of positive global economic change. Browsers, bandwidth, and the maturation of protocols for worldwide information exchange have "flattened the playing field" from a competitive standpoint while the rise of mobile telephony has brought more than a billion people into a seamless global communication network. Each of these innovations yielded new efficiencies that work to the benefit of companies—and entire economies—both large and small.

But Friedman's vision is enhanced by rose-colored glasses. The participants at the International Research Forum debated and advanced a more nuanced point of view that might best be described as a corollary to Friedman's principle. If the world is indeed flat, they suggested, then it is also tilted. Jobs, growth, and wealth are sliding down both the value chain and the development curve, from the peaks of Europe and the United States, toward less-developed nations in Asia, Africa, and South America. The tenor of the discussion was dominated by the tension implicit in this metaphor—how could the developed world help less-advantaged nations climb this slope without sliding down it themselves? They face mounting competition from many new corners of the globe that were mainly consumers of technology, not major producers.

India and China have most famously taken advantage of the flattening world to leverage their highly educated workforces (India and China annually graduate more engineers than even the U.S.), rapidly improving technological infrastructures, low wage scales, and even their differences in time zones, to become important players in the global economy. Chinese PC-maker Lenovo is now one of the world's largest, after purchasing IBM's PC division, while, in India, firms like Infosys, the Tata Group, and Bharti now compete or collaborate with global blue-chips such as SAP, Nokia, and even Wal-Mart, at home and in the heart of Europe.

The session was dominated by the discussion of how Europe—which lacks the socioeconomic infrastructure of the U.S. and Silicon Valley—will compete in the tilted world. Participants talked at length about possible responses from both a policy and competitive standpoint. If the bottom of the global value chain is inevitably headed down the slope, then how can Europe use ICT to add still more value to products and services at the top of the chain?

But the developing world faces an even stiffer challenge at the bottom of the slope. To fully tap the potential of ICT as India and China have done (barely, when one considers their success stories within the context of their populations as a whole), these nations must improve their communications infrastructure, achieve higher levels of education for their people, and identify and encourage the development of both affordable hardware and software.

Considering the lack of even the most basic infrastructure, such as power and telecom grids (not to mention food and fresh drinking water), any efforts to accelerate development via ICT must focus on opportunities to leapfrog existing technologies with vastly simpler, more affordable, and more rugged solutions, rather than simply import what currently exists in the developed world. How can these technologies address the needs of these emerging regions? What technology breakthroughs are required? How can governments, corporations, and institutions in the developed world help peers in the developing one so that both might prosper? And what are the limits to what ICT technologies can do?

The participants touched upon each of these questions during what quickly became a freewheeling debate about whether to foreground the anxieties of Europe or the epic struggle facing the developing world. This

---

European ICT Giants

(as ranked in the 2006 *Fortune* Global 500, *http://money.cnn.com/ magazines/fortune/global500/2006/industries/*)

Siemens (22)

Deutsche Telekom (54)

Vodafone (66)

France Télécom (71)

Telefónica (108)

Nokia (131)

Telecom Italia (141)

Royal Philips Electronics (145)

BT (162)

Vivendi (239)

L.M. Ericsson (319)

Alcatel (411)

Royal KPN (457)

---

chapter will follow the flow of this debate and use it to illustrate examples of how ICT is creating new opportunities and hope at the top and bottom of the tilted world, with a new mission for Europe and hard-charging entrepreneurs in India, and new strategies for leapfrogging millions of Africans out of poverty.

Europe: Sliding Down the Slippery Slope

Fabio Colasanti, the Director General for Information Society and Media at the European Commission, opened the session with a review and critique of the European Union's failure over the last seven years to galvanize support for ICT as the key mechanism for economic growth.

He had overseen the EC's so-called "Lisbon strategy," conceived in 2000 after an EC summit in the Portuguese capital had concluded that steps needed to be taken to jump-start growth once the macro-economic housecleaning required for unification—deficit reductions, industry consolidation, and so on—had been achieved. ICT was identified as the greatest opportunity for doing so, and Europe's leaders proclaimed the goal of becoming "the most dynamic and competitive

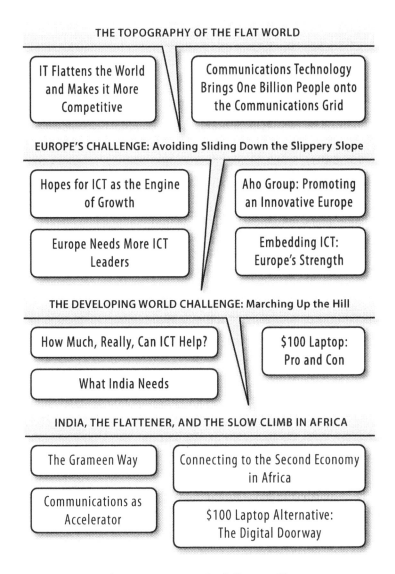

THE TOPOGRAPHY OF THE FLAT WORLD

IT Flattens the World and Makes it More Competitive

Communications Technology Brings One Billion People onto the Communications Grid

EUROPE'S CHALLENGE: Avoiding Sliding Down the Slippery Slope

Hopes for ICT as the Engine of Growth

Aho Group: Promoting an Innovative Europe

Europe Needs More ICT Leaders

Embedding ICT: Europe's Strength

THE DEVELOPING WORLD CHALLENGE: Marching Up the Hill

How Much, Really, Can ICT Help?

$100 Laptop: Pro and Con

What India Needs

INDIA, THE FLATTENER, AND THE SLOW CLIMB IN AFRICA

The Grameen Way

Connecting to the Second Economy in Africa

Communications as Accelerator

$100 Laptop Alternative: The Digital Doorway

Figure 5-1. IT as a Tool Chapter Map

knowledge-based economy in the world" by 2010, which would be marked by a 3 percent average annual economic growth and the creation of 20 million jobs. These publicly stated goals fit so neatly with the zeitgeist that Lisbon became popularly known as Europe's "dot.com summit."

 **Fabio Colasanti** currently serves as European Commission Director General for Information Society and Media. From 2000 to 2002, he was Director General of the European Commission's Enterprise Directorate General. Prior to that appointment, he was Deputy Head of the Office of European Commission President Romano Prodi and a Director in the European Commission's Budget Directorate General, with responsibility for the Resources Directorate. From 1988 to the end of 1995, Mr. Colasanti served successively as Head of the Economic Forecasts and Macroeconomic Policy Analysis units of the Commission's Directorate General for Economic and Financial Affairs. Meanwhile, he studied local development issues in the U.S. during a three-month trip across 18 states, thanks to an Eisenhower Fellowship in 1992.

Before returning to the Directorate General Economic and Financial Affairs, Mr. Colasanti was a member of the Commission's Spokesman's Group with responsibility for economic and monetary affairs, regional policy, credit and investment, and small- and medium-sized enterprises (the portfolios of Commissioners Aloïs Pfeiffer and Abel Matutes), from 1985 to the end of 1987. From October 1977 to 1984, he worked as an economist in the Commission's Directorate General for Economic and Financial Affairs. And from 1971 to 1977, he held various positions with Italcable Spa of Rome, which is now part of Telecom Italia.

Mr. Colasanti holds degrees in economics from the University of Rome and the College of Europe in Bruges. He works regularly in English and French and is fluent in German and Spanish.

But these proclamations ultimately had less to do with growth and productivity than with what Mr. Colasanti described as Europe's internal "redistributive debate" at the time. "It was [about] the employers trying to obtain from the unions—from the workers—more structural reforms and more flexibility, and [left] the labor workforce feeling that this was a loss," he said.

There was a hope that the spread of ICT would guarantee the flexibility and efficiency needed to compete in a global marketplace, but without damaging the Union's social contract with its citizens.

It recalled Europe's post-war situation in the 1950s, when rapid economic growth eased the burden of the heavy taxation needed for reconstruction.

"At the time of the Lisbon summit," Mr. Colasanti said, "many people felt that embracing ICT would be the way to achieve faster growth, and with faster growth the demand for structural reforms might not have been eliminated, but at least it would have lost some of its intensity."

The bursting of the dot-com era's stock market bubbles only a week after the Lisbon summit tainted ICT in the short term, he supposed,

"Growth is always the loser."

but the much larger challenge facing Europe is the mindset of its aging populations and their leaders, who—like any older, affluent individuals—prize security, stability, and solidarity far above growth. "They need growth for everything they want, but they just don't realize it. And in all the trade-offs that are agreed upon, growth is always the loser."

What has changed since Lisbon, Mr. Colasanti offered, is that European politicians have finally realized that "ICT is not an alternative to structural reforms." ICT amplifies economic growth in economies that have already liberalized, but cannot substitute for the liberalization itself. "And for some, that discovery had led to a lot of disappointment."

McKinsey Director **Claudia Funke** was more succinct when she addressed Mr. Colasanti's opening remarks. "We are in a very, very bad condition." Europe comprises a third of the world economy, measured in GDP, she pointed out, but its position in ICT and related high-tech industries is just half that. "Given that this is a future-oriented industry and that this is the first early warning indicator for what is going to happen to the other sectors, this is a real disaster."

She quickly ticked off the factors that led to her dour assessment:

- Europe has a dearth of global ICT leaders; the few within its ranks include SAP, Nokia, and Philips (although several participants argued this list should be supplemented with regionally dominant telecoms such Deutsch Telekom and T-Systems)

- A lack of management talent and entrepreneurs in these industries

- Too little and too unfocused investments in research and development, in both the public and private sectors

- The failure on the part of Europe's governments to drive over-all growth through their own, large-scale adoption of ICT

"We are so concerned within McKinsey about the future of that industry that we really feel something needs to be done, and not in 10 years, but sooner rather than later," Ms. Funke said.

"If I thought it was hopeless, I wouldn't be sitting here. But it is five minutes to midnight."

"If there is not high-volume demand" in their home countries, stimulated by government spending and adoption, "how [can] we have a Europe-based global high-tech or ICT industry?" she argued, adding ominously, "if I thought it was hopeless, I wouldn't be sitting here. But it is five minutes to midnight."

Mr. Colasanti concluded his remarks with the hope that the EC will learn from its past mistakes and will do the utmost to sell its citizens on the social, as well economic, benefits of ICT. He mentioned a handful of initiatives in the areas of "e-health, e-government, public services, and security" as examples, as well as a few models of what not to do when attempting to align public opinion with scientific fact: "I hope we will not repeat the mistake in terms of presentation that we made with genetically modified food or nuclear power," he said.

Prof. José Luis Encarnação, Professor of Computer Science at Technical University Darmstadt and a specialist in computer graphics, picked up this thread in his statements, which followed both Mr. Colasanti's and Ms. Funke's remarks. Drawing upon the reports and conclusions of the EC's Information Society Technologies Advisory Group (ISTAG), Prof. Encarnação made the case that advancing ICT—and, by extension, economic growth—within the EU depended upon selling the benefits to three constituencies, in succession: society, governments, and industry. If the public believes in its benefits, he said, "politics will follow with frameworks, legislation and, hopefully, positive conditions. Then, industry will be responsible for transposition, market opportunity, generation of jobs, new business models, and developing new market opportunities."

All of this, of course, is easier said than done. The first challenge is successfully framing the benefits of ICT in terms the public can understand, Prof. Encarnação explained. Advances in specific industries such as health care or transportation can be explained in concrete terms such as saving lives and billions of euros. Not only have ICT advocates failed, so far, to illustrate the steady integration of these technologies into almost all industries, but also how "we can integrate innovation into the production process. This will delay outsourcing to low-cost labor regions, and would guarantee that we have jobs in a certain area for a certain product for a longer period. And that, of course, society understands."

ICT advocates have failed to indicate how "we can integrate innovation into the production process."

Prof. Encarnação called for direct spending in ICT research to "stimulate the development of lead markets," including the areas mentioned in the 2006 Aho Group Report (see sidebar), including health, aging populations, and transportation. He also highlighted the need for tax incentives and structural investment. But most importantly, he offered a short list of technologies and research areas that he judged to be critical to Europe's competitiveness in the era of globalization.

With elements of the value chain becoming commoditized and outsourced and offshored to India, China, and the next bottom rungs in the developing world, it was apparent to all of the forum participants present that maintaining Europe's position at the top of this slippery slope would depend upon defining and creating the ICT that would reside at the top of the next generation value chain, rather than attempting to rebuild a technology platform that it had never really owned. "We cannot reproduce Intel or Oracle here," declared one participant.

Professor José Luis Encarnação was born in Portugal and has been living in the Federal Republic of Germany since 1959. Since 1975, he has been Professor for Computer Science at the Technical University Darmstadt and is Head of the Chair Graphical-Interactive Systems (TUD-GRIS). Under Professor Encarnação's leadership, the INI-GraphicsNet was established. This institutional network with more than 350 staff members, over 500 part-time student employees, and a budget of more than 40 million euros is one of the global key players in the area of visualization technologies, new media, and new forms of communications and interaction. Beyond this he founded a private enterprise, the INI-GraphicsNet Investitions Holding GmbH, and is one of the sponsors of the INI-GraphicsNet Foundation.

Professor Encarnação holds a Dipl.-Ing. and Dr.-Ing. in Electrical Engineering from the Technical University of Berlin. He is author or coauthor of more than 500 publications and articles, and is Editor-in-Chief of *Computers & Graphics*, published by Elsevier Science. Since July 2001, he has been Chairman of the Information and Communication Group of the Fraunhofer Society, with 15 institutes in 10 locations in Germany with a staff of 3,000 people and an annual budget of €190 million.

Professor Encarnação has received numerous awards, including the German Federal Service Cross, the German Federal Service Cross First Class, Portugal's "Ordem Militar de Sant'Iago de Espada," and the Fraunhofer Medal. In addition, he has received honorary professorships from the Zhejiang University in Hangzhou, China, and the Universidade Estadual de Campinas in São Paulo, Brazil, as well as honorary doctorates from the Universidade Técnica de Lisboa, the University of Rostock, and the Universidade do Minho.

Debating this list of ICT priorities and objectives was not only the focus of Prof. Encarnação's talk, but also of the participants present, who argued and advocated for their own proposals during the rebuttal and question period. A summary of both Prof. Encarnação's and participants' suggestions follows.

Creating an Innovative Europe: The Aho Group Report

In the aftermath of the Hampton Court Summit in October 2005, European leaders set a new agenda meant to address the challenges they faced in the wake of increasing globalization. Four experts, chaired by former Finnish prime minister Esko Aho, issued a reported in January 2006 outlining a four-pronged strategy to drastically stimulate research and innovation "before it is too late" and calls for a "Pact for Research and Innovation" to be signed by European political, business, and cultural leaders to demonstrate their commitment to the task ahead. The report declared there was a large and growing gulf between the political rhetoric about a "knowledge society" and the reality of the EU's budgetary priorities. The authors proposed the following:

- Fostering innovation-friendly markets that would spur companies to invest in R&D. To this end, they argued for coherent regulation, ambitious standardization, driving demand through public procurement, and intellectual property rights on par with the U.S. and elsewhere.
- Making more resources available for research and innovation. The much-touted 3 percent of GDP target should be seen as an indicator of a more innovative Europe, not an end in itself. Existing resources would be reprioritized, and resources would be reassigned to the most promising projects. And the EU should triple R&D spending within its discretionary "Structural Funds" budget to 20 percent.
- Creating a new paradigm of "structural mobility" within Europe, with increased flexibility and adaptability in financial and organizational structures. This would include goals such as encouraging 10 percent of Europe's research workforce laboring on cross-disciplinary work (for example, scientists working with government) and dramatically increasing venture capital investment in the EU, which has fallen more than 90 percent since 2000 (from €9.6 billion to just €946 million.)
- Lastly, creating a European culture that celebrates innovation—a task that sounds easier than it is.

At the conclusion of Mr. Colasanti's opening comments, Siemens' Vice President of Information and Communications, **Dr. Hartmut Raffler,** offered his own company as an example of how ICT would determine the success or failure of any European corporation, in any field (or all of them, as Siemens seems to be). Siemens spends more than 5 billion euros on R&D annually, he said, with half of that figure allotted for the projects of 30,000 software engineers on staff. "Sixty percent of our business is influenced by software, all of our business segments are heavily

"ICT has influence on all economic sectors."

influenced by ICT, and IT increasingly determines the functionality of our products. So ICT has influence on all economic sectors."

Dr. Raffler also called for participants to recognize the opportunities implicit in what he termed "the fragmentation of systems." The decomposition of enterprise applications, and other previously monolithic architectures, into smaller fragments and more flexible components will give European companies a chance to compete via business process innovation, rather than on price. The fragmentation of the value chain not only makes offshoring possible at the low end, but it also allows for the periodic reinvention of the value chain at the very top.

The disadvantage of fragmentation, he offered, is fragility, which is why further R&D is a necessity in the areas of software architecture, distributed systems, infrastructure, knowledge management, and security.

Picking up where Dr. Raffler left off, a participant argued that Europe's strongest industries, such as aviation and auto manufacturing, have done the best job historically of embedding ICT in their value chains. "Look at our car industry while all the car makers in the U.S. go downhill," he said. "Look at the airline industry. Lufthansa has been using ICT from the beginning—they have the most modern systems and were the first to introduce wireless Internet in flight. Lufthansa is flourishing while the U.S. airlines go downhill."

The application of ICT to industries outside of the typical high-tech sectors offers perhaps the best blueprint for economic growth. "It brings together the strengths in ICT with the manufacturing base here, and also the customers. We have to look at companies like Siemens, or our telecom industry." Europe should focus on the design and integration of complex, highly efficient systems, rather than attempt to build tools or protect commodity services.

Active@Work

Reacting to Mr. Colasanti's remarks on the aging of European societies (and Dr. Raffler's contention that there is an opportunity there), Prof. Lutz Heuser raised the issue of retaining knowledge from an increasingly older and retiring workforce. ICT should be used, he argued, to better capture their knowledge and retain it. Such knowledge might be useful not only for the economy of Germany, for instance, but for those of other, less-developed nations, as well—including those, perhaps, that are "very young and getting younger every year," in his words.

Prof. Heuser described one such effort to do just that: the EC's "Active@Work" effort in Finland, Germany, and Italy. In the German program, of which SAP and Deutsche Bank are sponsors, the goal is to motivate selected top performers above the age of 55 to share their institutional memory before reaching the beginning of retirement age five years later, when their knowledge may be irrevocably lost. "We have to ask ourselves," Prof. Heuser said, "how we can represent this knowledge in systems so that we can transform and deliver it to others in the next generation."

McKinsey's Ms. Funke agreed as well, pointing to British Telecom's Global Services unit as a prime example of integrated telecommunication and IT services "that you do not see elsewhere in the world." Companies that have also combined traditional European strengths in luxury and design—as luxury conglomerates such as LVMH, Gucci Group, and Prada have already done—could also prove to be a model for other industries. "It's about figuring out in the other sectors where their strengths are and combining them with ICT rather than trying to replicate something, which is lost anyhow," she said.

"ICT embedded into products seems to be what we all are talking about, and not ICT on its own," argued **Prof. Lutz Heuser.** Citing one of SAP CEO Henning Kagermann's speeches, he noted that 80 percent of the innovation in the automotive industry is software-driven. If that is indeed true, he argued, then what would appear to be Europe's great weakness—its lack of ICT giants and their legions of developers—is actually its position of strength. "It's clear that there are more software

Insourcing: Bringing Call Centers Back Home

Mark Kobayashi-Hillary, the author of *Outsourcing to India: The Offshore Advantage,* and coauthor of the forthcoming *Global Services: Moving to a Level Playing Field,* raises a corollary point. Mr. Kobayashi-Hillary takes a balanced view of outsourcing and offshoring, noting that the pendulum is beginning to swing back in cases where it makes more sense, such as in call centers.

"One of the important things worth remembering is that both America and Europe are exporting a lot more services to the world than they are importing them. Don't just look at 'software development' as a category, for example, but at software development in providing technical services to the legal or consulting or architectural professions. You'll find that the United Kingdom is exporting these specific technological resources more than a place like India is. Industry experience and local knowledge of how that industry works is the key value-add. Someone who can pick up a keyboard and write a bit of Java code is certainly portable, but every industry needs technology that must be combined with the particulars of how that industry functions, and that requires local expertise."

"We're already moving beyond the cost play here in Europe. A phenomenon we've already seen is the return of some voice-based call centers. The call center industry in the U.K. is actually growing at a pretty healthy rate. Why? Because companies are more interested in how they interact with their customers rather than reducing costs by moving jobs offshore. For many smart companies, that first touch point with the consumer will be the call center, and so they don't see a point in outsourcing it."

developers right now in the embedded environment than in all of the software companies you can think of put together." Not even Microsoft, Oracle, or SAP can marshal the ICT resources of a Siemens, Alcatel, Philips, or Ericsson. The question is: how do they best leverage their sheer advantage in numbers?

Prof. Encarnação, whose speech came after the comments listed above, grouped all of these assertions under his own heading of "agile manufacturing," which once again refers to the question of "how can we put more innovation in the product itself so that production cannot be outsourced so easily?" The reorganization of global value chains will lead to a fundamental shift in the structure of corpora-tions—"what we'll see all over the world," he said, "are borderless digital ecosystems."

To support this shift, he stressed, the EC and the relevant stakeholders needed to develop strategies and agendas for research that will bridge the gaps to the next ICT paradigm, that

The Future: "What we'll see all over the world are borderless digital ecosystems."

of so-called "ambient intelligence" (in Europe), also known as "ubiq-uitous computing" (in the U.S.). "If we succeed in making the vision of ambient intelligence happen," he concluded, "then we have the motor to develop the creativity and innovation needed to respond to the dif-ferent social challenges that we are addressing and have been discuss-ing here."

The Developing World: Marching Up The Hill

Dr. Peter Kürpick rose to challenge the Euro-centric slant of the proceedings. "I think we have two maybe fundamentally different issues here," he began. "One was, as Prof. Encarnação said, the high-end 'Western World.' And the other end of the story is: 'how do I spread this into emerging countries?' Because reaching the hundreds of mil-lions of people there is a different story than tackling the challenge of staying high-end in a specific country or in a specific region."

With only 15 minutes remaining in the session, the assembled par-ticipants made a valiant effort to catalog the challenges, success stories, and paths forward offered by the developing world. But even if the entire session had been given over to questions surrounding India, Africa, and beyond, the International Research Forum couldn't possibly tackle these topics with the full breadth and depth of thought each one deserves. In the limited time available, however, the speakers were able to at least touch upon enough of these issues to warrant a more thorough explora-tion in these pages. Their comments have been expanded upon with a series of one-on-one interviews conducted with selected experts in the field to create a collage of opinions and commentary and a handful of the most pertinent issues, including rapid economic development—practically straight from a subsistence economy to a post-industrial one—

"Developing countries will need to quickly find their voice if globalization is to be a more inclusive and sustainable force."

and education, the great twin hopes for the use of ICT in the developing world.

Growing market-based economies are the most effective in reducing poverty, the neo-liberal thinking goes, which leads to wiser, more sustainable use of environmental resources. In theory, ICT can enable indigenous industries—even those that are rural and craft-based—to tap into larger markets and command better prices than before. Even farmers can benefit from improved access to information about crop prices, transportation services, and the weather. As it has already proven in the developed world, ICT has the power to help even tiny producers achieve the advantages of disintermediation—replacing the social and economic friction of brokers, distributors, and other middlemen (including loan sharks) with more or less direct participation in efficient markets.

Jump-starting education has long been seen as the other key goal, as sustained economic development isn't possible without a population capable of climbing up the value chain. ICT has been seen by some educators as the only mechanism for delivering educational materials (in digital form) to the hundreds of millions of children too poor or too isolated to receive textbooks. The Internet can step in with "distance learning"—the infrastructure of students without a teacher being physically present, since teachers are another scarce commodity in vast swaths of the world. Computer-based teaching methods can drill students in everything from the classic "three Rs" (reading, writing, and arithmetic) to sophisticated simulation tools necessary for an education in science, mathematics, or engineering.

For all its promise as a catalyst, however, ICT cannot be transplanted into newly industrializing economies without a great deal of thought, planning, and effort. Many well-intentioned and

What India Needs

Nandan M. Nilekani, cofounder and CEO of Infosys, one of India's largest software companies, is one of the most ardent and eloquent advocates for India's software industry. Mr. Nilekani is also the man who informed Thomas Friedman that "the playing field is being leveled." To add a complementary layer to the discussion from the forum, the authors spoke to him about India and its future: "Access, combined with the fact that knowledge-based services can be done from anywhere that's wired, has essentially provided work from anywhere on the planet. That's really the fundamental premise of the so-called flat world. That flattening of access translates into my ability to serve customers and create value in a way I could not have done 30 years ago. That's the source of the growth of the whole outsourcing industry in India. It's entirely because people who couldn't participate in the global workforce gained access to technology. But there are four things that must happen in order for India to become a more developed nation."

"One requirement, if you really want to change India, is universal education. In India we don't really have universal literacy. If you are illiterate, you can't perform a lot of jobs in this part of the world. And unless we are able to make every person literate, you have barred them from the marketplace."

"The second thing is health care. Because one of the challenges of poverty is malnutrition. And if it's malnutrition at a young and formative age, your children will not grow to their full intellectual potential."

"The third is access to jobs. Unless you have access to the ability to earn an income, you can't really prosper. The challenge that a country like India faces is a very young population, with 10 to 14 million young people joining the workforce every year. And they are likely to be extremely alienated if they are not able to participate in the growth. So if we don't give them jobs, we get shut out of this global economy."

"The fourth is urbanization, a phenomenon that was happening in the West in the 19th and 20th centuries, but in countries like China and India it's happening now. The difference is that it's happening much faster, at a rate of 1 percent a year. And it's happening in an era of universal suffrage and labor rights. Which means that if a lot of people migrate to the city, and they all want to work, they can essentially influence the way the city develops. What happens in India is you have a

(continued on next page)

(continued from previous page)
lot of migration from the rural areas to the cities. So they all come to the cities and the cities don't have coping mechanisms to deal with the influx, which starts the slums. And slums are a common feature of all third-world countries."

"So unless you resolve these problems, unless you give everybody access to healthcare, to education, to jobs, and to public services like water and transportation, then it's really difficult to argue that you can reach the developed world."

well-financed attempts to parachute high-technology tools into developing economies have ended in catastrophic failure and even societal upheaval.

"There's lots and lots of equipment that's been sent overseas to the developing countries and that is useless," says **Lee Felsenstein,** an engineer who has designed ICT gear for use in remote, undeveloped areas. "Mostly, that's because it was never designed to be sufficiently rugged in the environment in question."

But the most ambitious effort yet to leverage ICT as a leapfrog technology is about to step onto the scene: the "$100 Laptop" (or "HDL") produced by the "One Laptop Per Child" (OLPC) project. Founded by a handful of MIT professors and led by MIT Media Lab founder Nicholas Negroponte, OLPC has been backed by a number of technology giants including the chip maker AMD, Google, Red Hat, and many others. Negroponte and his team are adamant in their belief that the $100 Laptop (which was colloquially named after its eventual cost to produce) will transform education in the developing world.

The engineering and design of the HDL (see "Inside the Hundred-Dollar Laptop") at least explicitly addresses many of the major questions looming around how best to deploy these technologies—all of which were originally created and produced by companies in the so-called North. How can they be best adopted by the less developed countries of the South, considering:

- How many PCs, priced at even $100 apiece, are feasible for a nation with little food, medicine, or fresh water to acquire when millions of its citizens survive on $1 or less each day?

- How can such machines be operated in locations where there are no electrical outlets supplying kilowatts of power 24/7, or where high levels of dust, heat, and humidity are the norm?

- And even if these machines survive, who will maintain them in the countryside?

- What kind of software is needed to serve users who may not be literate in English, or literate, period? Can specialized user interfaces be helpful?

- Must individual students each have their own computers, or are they better off being shared with the community?

- Is the PC-as-we-know-it even the best platform for the developing world? Isn't the most ubiquitous computing platform the mobile telephone? As a low-cost, low-power, easily provisioned communications technology, wouldn't it be a more appropriate and economically sustainable choice of technology?

- And should developing nations strive to foster their own IT industries, or can they benefit merely as consumers of IT goods and services that are developed far from their shores?

This last question touches on one of the most, if not *the* most, important ICT-related challenge facing the entire development movement: how can developing nations meaningfully participate in the governance of global ICT issues?

Lacking a say in the fast-evolving international regime that defines critical policies in these areas—such as intellectual property rights, privacy, market access, and the management of the electromagnetic spectrum and the Internet domain name space—developing nations

---

Inside the Hundred-Dollar Laptop

- Chip maker Marvell supplied a wireless chip that includes its own onboard CPU and RAM, which enables each chip to function as its own wireless router. The goal is to use each laptop to create a "mesh network"—a non-structured network that pools together the bandwidth and power of its individual nodes. Each laptop will be able to create hotspots larger than the source signal and share files without a server.

- The custom-designed screen operates using either a 1,200 x 900 pixel grayscale mode that's readable in sunlight or a lower-resolution backlit color screen. To conserve power, the screen uses LCDs rather than fluorescents, and the grayscale mode isn't backlit at all.

- The HDL has replaced spinning hard drives with solid-state flash memory to reduce power consumption. Chip maker AMD has also provided custom chips that fine-tune the laptop's overall consumption as well. The goal is to keep the CPU off 80 percent of the time, dropping its power needs to 2 watts, instead of the typical laptop's 25 watts.

- For increased ruggedness, the HDL is both water- and dust-resistant, uses flash memory instead of a hard drive, and is made of polystyrene and rubber.

- The hand crank that appeared in earlier prototypes is long gone, but California's Squid Labs has built a hand-pull generator with the goal of gaining 10 minutes of juice for every minute of pulling. Other manual methods of recharging the batteries are still being considered.

---

will remain at a severe, perhaps even crippling disadvantage. In fact, their failure to benefit fully from ICT may well threaten all nations as well. A society's failure to harness ICT will all but doom it to marginalization or even exile from the global economy, and that exile will in turn fuel a rise in poverty, human misery, environmental degradation, and, arguably, terrorist activity.

India: The World Flattener

C. K. Prahalad's book *The Fortune at the Bottom of the Pyramid* documents many case studies from India. Several of these were discussed at the forum, and these case studies showed a pattern that aids in understanding when ICT-led initiatives cause social and economic benefits.

The Argument for the Hundred-Dollar Laptop

Greg Wyler is the founder of Terracom, Rwanda's largest telecommunications company. In less than three years, Terracom succeeded in installing over 350 km of fiber-optic cables connecting Rwanda's largest cities, Kigali and Butare, and has established nationwide wireless broadband with the help of solar-powered cellular towers and EVDO 3G broadband. Because Rwanda is one of the first governments to submit an order for OLPC laptops, Terracom will be helping to implement them "in the near future," Mr. Wyler says.

"Our experience shows Nicholas is right about children learning on their own," says Mr. Wyler. "He's right that if you give a kid a computer, they will figure it out, it responds to their input, and they in turn respond and grow along with it. For the child it is playing, but it is also learning."

"Many of us think of schools based upon our historical experience, for instance in the USA or Europe. We do not imagine a one-room schoolhouse, no doors, no lights, and many times no teacher. In many developing countries, the teachers themselves have a very limited education and the kids and teachers need access to extend their own knowledge, and the computer needs to be the child's so they feel they can play with it, modify it, and get to know it outside of a lesson plan."

"Internet infrastructure is crucial to a nation's development. One of the more frequent comments I hear is 'Why are you putting fiber-optic cables and Internet access into places that also need food, water, and antiviral drugs?' First, any large-scale distribution of these items requires an IT infrastructure to efficiently coordinate, distribute, and allocate, and second, the infrastructure helps to build businesses and education which create jobs and improve the countries' tax base to allow the country to become more self-sufficient."

"Rwanda has the talent. For example, a company named SolidWorks is one of the leaders in mechanical CAD drawings. They need people to create 3D objects from 2D drawings. We connected a technical school (ETO Gitarama) with fiber 70 kilometers from Kigali, and Solidworks sent an instructor and installed their CAD software. Now the kids are designing and rendering solid models on screen and they are starting a new company in Kigali to do 3D modeling of 2D images. Imagine—kids who didn't know what a screwdriver was are now rendering them. This is a small success story in the making, and it's proof that as the world gets smaller, and more connected, the more we can affect and help people."

The Argument Against the Hundred-Dollar Laptop

Lee Felsenstein, cofounder of the Fonly Institute, has openly criticized the OLPC project for what he sees as a dangerous degree of naiveté or even willful ignorance in the face of cultural or socioeconomic barriers. "The implementation plan is unworkable," he says, "based as it is on a naive faith in technology to change everything, including traditional social structures, and the very concept of education." Having ignored prior research and best practices, Mr. Felsenstein fears that the OLPC's backers will use their clout to win acceptance (and orders) from governments and large corporations without any input from children, their parents, or their teachers. When the project's utopian distribution plans inevitably run into difficulties, there is a real danger that the fallout could render any other attempts to introduce ICT in these countries "radioactive" for the foreseeable future. "OLPC is making a serious mistake for which other implementers will pay in the aftermath," he says.

Rather than impose a great technological leap forward by fiat, Mr. Felsenstein advocates a "fair trade" approach to introducing new tools in developing nations. Instead of just handing out the latest and greatest devices, a real effort is made to understand what local producers need to participate in the broader marketplace. From a purely ICT standpoint, that means figuring out what those potential users want and responding to their "pull" with systems shaped by their needs, as opposed to "pushing" technology on them. In practice, this might mean community-based approaches rather than individual ones. "I think of it in terms of one telecenter per village, versus one laptop per child," he says.

Like many of the engineers who designed early personal computers and sought to bring "appropriate technologies" to what was then called the Third World, Mr. Felsenstein took much inspiration from a 1974 book, *Tools for Conviviality* by social critic Ivan Illich. As Illich used the term, a convivial tool is, in part, highly effective yet doesn't demand heavy investments in training for those who wish to use or maintain it.

"Illich pointed out that as radio was expanded into Central America, within two years there were people there who knew how to fix it," Mr. Felsenstein recalls. "These people had never left their areas to go somewhere else and take training. They got their training right at the point of use, because the equipment was—fortuitously, I suppose—built and designed such that it could survive exploration."

(continued on next page)

(continued from previous page)

"That made the point to me that one had to take the same approach with computer technology," Mr. Felsenstein explains. "It's possible to design things so that they are more welcoming and accessible to people who are going to have to explore them in order to be able to maintain them. To a certain degree, you can make your design work along with normal, human tendencies for curiosity, and a certain number of people will actually pursue that curiosity. There has to be a kind of conceptual simplicity and integrity of the system, so that you can grasp some general principles readily, and these principles apply across the board."

While the OLPC fulfills these requirements at a hardware and engineering level, he says, they cannot overcome a highly nonconvivial design for the implementation. The project's leaders either falsely assume or fail to predict that the laptop's sudden presence will transform how children learn, that families will not seek to use this valuable (in both a practical and monetary sense) tool on their own terms, and so on.

The notion that people in developing countries need higher levels of formal education to expand their use of ICT is a "red herring," Mr. Felsenstein declares. "It dates from efforts by early computer practitioners to distinguish themselves and raise their status. The idea that you need to have college education to use computers is ridiculous. Where does one use the particular things that one learned in a college education in using the computer? And the answer is, nowhere. The whole issue of education is, to me, a comparative nonstarter. The education that goes on is one person teaching another. You have to be receptive to that."

This pattern was later defined by Deependra Moitra as "constraint-based development," or in other words, ICT technologies that Indian entrepreneurs and companies had adopted or modified to address their own economic needs and realities. The thrust of Prahalad's book is that there is an enormous fortune—in the form of pent-up consumer demand and aggregate savings—in the billions of people who possess four- or even three-figure incomes. The key to unlocking this fortune, which he suggested and others have proved since, is to reinvent business models for a marketplace that is infinitely broad but only a few dollars deep.

"I am a technological adventurer," **Lee Felsenstein** has said about himself, "The problem is getting anyone to pay for it."

In fact, Mr. Felsenstein, a hardware engineer, is best known for his long-standing effort at demystifying technology and giving more people, in the U.S. and abroad, access to the benefits of ICT. In the 1970s, he helped run the Community Memory Project, a public-access electronic bulletin board in Berkeley, Calif. Later, he designed the Osborne 1 computer, the first "luggable" computer and a huge market success. Today, he heads the Fonly Institute, a consulting R&D organization in Palo Alto, Calif., that creates "sustainable systems that facilitate economic self-development in rural and underserved communities." Fonly—the name derives from "if only"—has received much attention for a bicycle-powered ICT system it designed for refugee villages in remote areas of Laos.

It was pointed out that even financial institutions like the micro-credit pioneering Grameen Bank—founded in 1976 in Bangladesh by 2006 Nobel Peace Prize winner Muhammad Yunus—have had to reinvent themselves, Dr. Kumar pointed out. The Grameen Bank pioneered the practice of lending the equivalent of only a few dollars, often without collateral, to anyone who asked. Perhaps counter-intuitively, the borrowers' repayment rates have historically hovered above 98 percent. Over the past 30 years, the Grameen Bank has lent nearly $6 billion to 6.6 million borrowers, through 2,226 branches. The bank has since grown into more than two dozen enterprises, applying its constraint-based approach to education, energy, and yes, ICT (see "The Grameen Way"). Meanwhile, Western banks, led by Citi and its recently announced $100 million microfinance fund, are deploying a similar approach.

Reinvention is certainly a necessity for any ICT company seeking to do business in India. The typical adoption cycle of new technologies— led by early adopters willing to pay top dollar and followed by those willing to cross the metaphorical chasm—breaks down in a constrained

The Grameen Way

The Grameen Foundation sprang from Muhammad Yunus's efforts to apply the micro-credit model he developed at the Grameen Bank to other industries, notably ICT. The Grameen Foundation has set out to bring telephony to remote areas through the Village Phone program, which enables microfinance clients to operate mobile phone–based public telephone services in their villages—an effective, low-capital method for implementing technology in a way that is self-sustaining and that can help local farmers and laborers act more effectively in their own economic interests.

According to Tim Wood, Technical Project Manager at the Grameen Technology Center, Grameen believes that the best way to introduce new technologies to lesser-developed locales is to make sure they are supported by "sustainable business models."

Entrepreneurs participating in its Village Phone program act, in effect, as operators of their communities' public payphone. They borrow just enough money to purchase a standard cell phone and perhaps acquire a high-gain directional antenna that enables the phone to operate as far away as 35 km from a cellular base station. Using these phones on a pay-per-minute basis, their customers can call anywhere in the world. But the most valuable calls in the long run are those that enable the villages to participate in markets more effectively—to learn the current prices for crops, arrange for the transport of goods, and learn of job openings, for example. More than 7,000 operators have signed up so far, and the model has proven to be financially sustainable for the telecommunications company, the microfinance institutions, and the Village Phone operators.

Meanwhile, the Grameen Foundation developed PC-based accounting software for Grameen Bank's microfinance institutions—some 2,226 small-scale banking operations located in 43 countries that currently serve more than 6.6 million borrowers. This open source software helps lenders lower their cost of operations while improving efficiency and making the entire micro-credit project more effective in fostering sustainable development.

environment. One example mentioned was that of the Indian mobile phone market, which already numbers more than 100 million customers. (Amazingly, that figure represents only 10 percent of the potential market).

While it was stated that the monthly cost of a phone in Europe is about twenty euros, it became known that in India *lifetime* connectivity—free

 **Tim Wood,** Technical Project Manager of the Grameen Foundation, specializes in applying information technology to address the problems of poverty and health in developing countries. After 12 years at Microsoft working on software development, Tim spent two years consulting with the Bill & Melinda Gates Foundation looking at the intersection of Information Technology and Global Health. He joined the Grameen Technology Center in 2002 and pioneered replication of the Grameen Village Phone program, launching sustainable initiatives in Uganda and Rwanda and coauthoring the *Village Phone Replication Manual.* Tim brings a broad range of technical and business expertise, and a valued perspective on technology initiatives for developing countries.

incoming calls for a lifetime—can be purchased for just $20. How does this work from a revenue standpoint? The explanation is that you have certain fixed and variable costs with the average revenue per user multiplied by these numbers. Although people started with an assumption of telecom usage in the range of 5 million people, there are now over 100 million users, and their number is expected to reach 200 million in the next couple of years.

It was suggested that the same thing is happening in software, even in enterprise applications. ERP solutions costing less than $500 per month were available there from small, local vendors. These very simple solutions—essentially a handful of terminals for data hosting and entry along with the process mapping and implementation—are nonetheless appropriate for the small business owners who are beginning to flourish.

Two patterns emerge. First, a constraint can be turned into a challenge and from there into an opportunity. Secondly, the application of ICT can be tied to a specific context to avoid becoming entrapped in policy issues. Key to this is to use technology to specifically address the current situation.

Running parallel to the discussion on constraints was a debate over communication versus computing in the developing world, and the importance of the interface, especially when applied to educational uses. Several speakers exchanged criticism and support concerning optimal interface design for developing nations, offering anecdotes that lent credence to their particular point of view.

"The user interface is of utmost importance to make functionality available to the user in a simple way. This is true not only for emerging economies—it's a worldwide phenomenon," argued a participant. "I remember when Bill Gates visited us last year. He said that the whole PC business is plateauing, that the market is saturated. There are many situations where you don't want to deal with windows and folders on a screen; you just want to watch a certain video in the living room, for instance. You don't want to deal with the normal click-and-mouse interface for this. Perhaps for the next meeting [of the forum] one of the megatrends should be the intelligent end-user interface—making things simpler by using speech, gestures, and other, very natural modes of interaction."

"It's communications that brings the world closer together and it's communications that is the real accelerator here."

Dr. Ike Nassi, Senior Vice President at SAP Research, Americas, argued that communication was the thing, not the interface: "The tremendous growth that we've seen in India, for example, is driven from the networking communications side, not the device side. It's communications that brings the world closer together and it's communications that is the real accelerator here. The computers, that's a separate thing. It's important, but it's not the main driver."

The issue of developing nations as ICT producers versus consumers was itself consumed by the discussion of using scripting as a tool for these nations to begin lightweight ICT production. MIT's Michael Schrage had suggested as much in an earlier session, making the case that up to a fairly high level of functionality, scripting languages can produce programs at much lower cost than would be possible with traditional programming in languages such as C++ or Java.

"A technology can serve the consumer side of the game or it can help people take an active role."

But he threw water on the idea when several participants cited scripting as one way for developing nations to foster indigenous software industries. "A technology can serve the consumer side of the game or it can help people take an active role, and that's where I think pushing for the scripting will be useful," said Dr. Kürpick. "With scripting one can take an active role pretty fast. Unless you take an active role, you're just consuming, and it doesn't lift you up [economically] to much extent."

Mr. Schrage's response was to caution the participants that "the challenge the rise of scripting languages poses is that it can give many individuals and many organizations the belief that they're living with the 80:20 principle—that for 20 percent of the cost they're getting 80 percent of the value of SAP. And for some organizations that will be true, while for others it may be that missing 20 percent that makes all the difference [to their success]. Whatever complaints people may have about SAP's software, it's not that the software's not well thought out and not rigorously done. Scripting is an alternate methodology and I can say this, as a computer science person: I don't even know how I would train rigorous methodology in scripting languages."

To make his point, he then posed a rhetorical question to Mr. Rattner of Intel: "When you are looking at people who you want to hire, when you're looking at the community of researchers that you want to reach, what kind of development skills and innovation skills do you want them to have? Because if you need quick and dirty innovation, I want to do a script. With C++, it's going to be many things. It'll be dirty, but it ain't going to be quick."

Africa: The Slow Climb Ahead

The $100 Laptop has become the de facto champion for deploying ICT in Africa and other regions where ICT development is all but nonexistent. In Libya and Rwanda—the first confirmed customers of the HDL—the debate over ICT production versus consumption has been moot until now. Infrastructure is so poor and resources so scarce, that turning to a potentially revolutionary ICT solution to leapfrog over their neighbors, up the steep slope of the Tilted World, is as sound a strategy as any. "We believe you have to leverage the kids themselves," one of the designers of the laptop told the *New York Times*. "They're learning machines."

Two contrasting views of the HDL and its efficacy are presented as sidebars on the next few pages. But other alternatives for harnessing the power of ICT for education and remedial development do exist. In fact, the first person to raise the topic at the forum was **Dr. Mandi S. Mzimba,** Senior Science and Technology Representative to Europe for South Africa's National Department of Science and Technology. Dr. Mzimba said that her country has already built a "fairly strong ICT sector on the back of mobile telephony," but growth in the sector has been hampered by a lack of local content and local industry.

"We have what we call a second economy, which is the more informal, poverty-stricken, socioeconomic problem economy characterized by low education, unemployment, and many social problems," Dr. Mzimba explained. "This second economy is a very large section of our overall economy, existing alongside a thriving, so-called first-world economy. What we need is to find ways to bridge that divide between the two."

She described an attempt to facilitate access to ICT and "to reach those who are traditionally unreachable" through a project named "the Digital Doorway." The ruggedized four-sided kiosks—with each side containing a small screen and keyboard—run on an open source OS similar to the HDLs and are connected to the Internet. The Digital Doorway "challenges conventional notions about introducing ICT, because it uses a minimally invasive approach. People must be able to use ICT at a very low-tech level, but with a high-tech load," Dr. Mzimba said.

Since 2002, the program has distributed 25 of the kiosks in public spaces to provide free and open Internet access in poor communities. An additional 50 kiosks are to be rolled out in 2007. "There is no supervision or training required, which significantly lowers the cost of

Dr. Mandi Mzimba is Senior Science and Technology Representative to Europe for South Africa's National Department of Science and Technology. In this role, she actively promotes and strengthens research and development in a bilateral cooperation with the European Commission and facilitates investment into scientific infrastructure and major research programs that address South African needs.

Dr. Mzimba previously served as Senior Executive at the Council for Geoscience, and as a Deputy Director for the National Department of Health, Pretoria and is responsible for the development of district health systems, for example the development of systems for measuring and monitoring the health status of South African citizens. Prior to that, Dr. Mzimba held positions with the South African Institute for Medical Research, Johannesburg; the University of Leeds; Libby's UK, a parent company of Nestle South Africa; and Swaziland Fruit Canners, Swaziland.

Dr. Mzimba holds a BSc (Honours) in Biochemistry from the University of Ibadan, Nigeria; an M.B.A. from Wits Business School; and both an M.Sc. in Clinical Biochemistry and a Ph.D. in Clinical Biochemistry from University of Leeds. She is a founding director of Imvuno Holdings (Pty) Ltd., a women's investment company. She has served on the board of Ikemeleng Molewa Consolidated Investments, Condomi SA, Protec, and PetroSA. In addition, she has been a member of the executive committees of the National Science and Technology Forum (NSTF) and the South African Research and Innovation Management Association (SARIMA).

the whole intervention and it allows community members to interact with the technology on their own terms and in their own language," she said, adding "everybody has the cognitive ability to master a new technology, but it doesn't replace the need to equip the schools with computers, and to equip the hospitals with computers."

Conclusion

The big questions in IT will always be with us. How can we share data securely? How do we create truly private systems? What is coming in the next few years that will turn IT on its ear?

In this book we have attempted to bring the reader into the rooms of the International Research Forum to listen in on some of the best minds of the IT world discuss the past, present, and future of the computing experience. We have also tried to bring some order to the thinking that occurred, and, where possible, lead the discussion in useful directions. Because of the breathtaking scope of the ideas covered, meeting both goals has proved a tremendous challenge.

The authors feel that they have captured the discussion competently and extended it in interesting ways. This chapter examines some of the ideas that occurred to the authors while writing the book that may be of use to those of us who spend our lives studying and building technology and putting it to work to achieve results.

While few of us have the occasion to work on anything that involves Web 2.0, IT security, real world awareness, or IT as a tool for growth and development in one single project or even in one year, all of us will encounter issues related to these trends in our daily work. We will encounter Web 2.0 through mashups that have been cobbled together and wonder if they are secure. We will walk through stores that tag our purchases with RFIDs and weigh the benefits of lower prices against possible threats to privacy. We may contribute to charities that pursue technology growth through "One Laptop Per Child" and wonder whether it is the right approach. If we've done our job in capturing the discussion of the forum, you should now have new ways to think about all these issues.

Looking back, we see one broad structure that appears repeatedly in the technologies and architectures discussed during the forum. While client/server technologies have existed since the 1970s, it seems that they have evolved to a new hub versus edge metaphor that aptly describes a number of new and up-and-coming technologies. With the advent of Internet technologies, the heavy lifting now happens at the hubs—the information stores that drive web sites, ecommerce, and other powerful mapping applications—while APIs and XML create an entire army of edge applications using mashups of various types of data to provide a completely new experience.

Living on the Edge

To better understand the hub-and-edge model used extensively throughout this book, let's look at one of the most prevalent and interesting examples. Google Maps is an online mapping service that offers an unadulterated view of the entire globe. Name an address or set of coordinates and you are there, in real time, watching the product of thousands, if not millions, of technologies. Google Maps melds satellite photography, advanced cartography, GPS, and complex programming algorithms to create a seamless mapping experience that has, until now, been unavailable to the common computer user.

This is the hub, the nexus of information. On a heat map Google Maps would be a white-hot core of data. But Google added one interesting twist. It offered an API to connect to and tweak that data. To understand the value of this API, consider the years leading up to Google Maps. Satellite data was costly and amazingly obtuse. Even John F. Kennedy's Cuban Missile Crisis photographs relied on a single plane flying low over the island of Cuba. Now, however, anyone—from a third-world farmer surveying his land to a student in Stockholm researching the Alps—has access to enough geographic data to fill a thousand atlases. Add in the power to create edge applications—to create a list of public toilets in New York City or San Francisco tagged to Google's maps or a simulation of the effects of global warming—and you have an entirely new paradigm for data creation, maintenance, and sharing.

Seeking to understand what is at the hub of a system and what is at the edge proved to be a consistent organizing theme of speakers at the conference, one that naturally emerged from the speaker's language. It seems that, when encountering any system, just asking a few simple questions to determine the difference between the hub and edge of a system's architecture helps clarify the nature of the system. Understanding the differences—and similarities—between hub-and-edge systems allows us to create an overarching vision of IT in the 21st century.

Web 2.0: It's about the Transactions

As we learned in Chapter 2, the concept of next-generation web interactivity is nebulous at best. It consists of a range of closely related technical developments including advanced Internet browsers, data-handling and data-passing protocols, and whole new ways of looking at information, unified by their tendency to improve as more people use them. Aiming the bright light of the hub-and-edge paradigm on this bramble, however, clears things up immensely.

Web 2.0 consists of content providers and content packagers. Everything in Web 2.0 comes from a basic core set of data points. Whether we are talking about Google's AdSense advertising system or Flickr's powerful photo-sharing software, the major players in Web 2.0 traffic in heavy-duty data.

On the edge, however, things are a bit more muddled. As devices and browsers attack this data, they read it and use it in odd and wonderful ways. Web 2.0 promises to mine value out of the Web that previously was untouchable due to problems with communication and system interoperability. Using a few basic commands, anyone can surf the hub data stores and create mashups of images, geographic data, and blog entries. Tag clouds create interesting new ways of understanding the worldwide interchange of ideas and give meaning to news in real time.

All of this would be impossible, however, without hub-and-edge architecture.

Web 2.0 came about, as we learned, due to the struggle between the hub and the edge. Users wanted to share data and create commerce systems while hubs—the large media companies and search organizations—wanted to monetize their wares. But in opening the doors to benevolent coders, the hub has turned a previously fuzzy and ambiguous edge into a thriving and potentially lucrative IT ecosystem. The ability of an API to provide powerful data and functionality and the way that a developer of a mashup can choose from hundreds of services from different sources has created a powerful new way of programming. The low cost of assembling such applications has tremendous commercial implications. Now, someone with an intimate understanding and access to a niche market can affordably create services for that market, allowing both the creator of the mashup and the service providers new sources of revenue. The way that community involvement can guide product development means that in many cases one product will evolve into many more. The ability to address such micro verticals suggests that the mechanisms of the long tail are not just a theory but will soon be an established fact. The key question is: how long will it take for mashups to migrate from the realm of interesting toys to robust platforms for transacting business? This remains to be seen.

Real World Awareness: A Million Little Sensors

A few short years ago, the responsibility to gather and process huge amounts of information fell to "big iron"—the massive mainframes we still remember from sci-fi movies—and their attendant operators. Small, powerful, and inexpensive computers were a pipe dream, and getting those computers to work together was almost impossible. Clearly, things have changed.

Hub-and-edge distinctions are easy to identify in the realm of real world awareness. Wal-Mart and other big retailers use RFID chips— essentially tiny transmitters or, in some cases, miniature computers—to track the boxes and pallets that pour through the system daily. The Department of Homeland Security is working on sensor buoys that bob in the water supplies of major cities and report back on poisonous conditions. Each one of these tiny sensors is on the edge of a powerful and far-reaching network while the hubs—often created by linking thousands of low-cost PCs together—process and maintain the data collected and, most importantly, report anomalies.

Without an architecture that places intelligence at the edge, many RWA systems would be impossibly complex. By offloading the sensor network to numerous tiny subsystems and sensors, IT shops are able to focus solely on the big picture. Rather than focusing on each subsystem as a separate device, these sensors act as a huge, organic network and ensure that the data stream to the hub is uninterrupted. Whereas we once felt that every PC on a network had to be equal in terms of storage capacity, power, and programming, the rise of inexpensive hardware has changed that concept completely. As we learned from the forum, the RWA systems have taken the guesswork out of data entry and given IT departments more freedom to focus on the big problems. Before RWA, data was manually entered; now RWA offers an automated methodology for capturing and handling data at the edge of complex systems, bypassing the human factor completely. This means more intelligence can be placed at the hub where the data is processed and reformatted for almost any purpose.

As RWA improves over time, the torrents of data these sensors produce will slowly be reduced to a trickle. Much of the data that comes from real world sensors is "spam." As these sensors become more intelligent and are able to weed out the important information from the unimportant, they will become even more useful.

IT Security: The Defender's Edge

Explaining IT security using the hub-and-edge metaphor is becoming increasingly simpler. The edge, in this case, consists of machines outside of the firewall serving data or web pages to the Internet cloud. The hubs, then, are the back-end systems that produce this data. Before the Internet, every computer was a hub. Creating an outside connection required a roomful of hardware and opened the machine to all sorts of potential mischief. Now, however, the edge devices can be placed outside of the firewall or between two firewalls in the so-called demilitarized zone if some protection is required.

The forum participants proposed a simple method for assessing the security of a device. MAST—which stands for Measurable, Available, Secure and Trusted—offers a paradigm that allows developers and system architects to assess the security of almost any device.

Security is a tradeoff between privacy and usability. The closer you get to 100 percent safety, the harder it is to create a usable system. Secure systems are expensive and should be placed in the hub of an organization. Things that must be secure must stay well inside the firewall while the edge can be quickly and easily populated by "worker bees" that provide outside interaction.

Just as hub devices can be as secure as possible, edge security must be loose enough to allow collaboration, unstructured communication, the sharing of data, and latitude for new applications to thrive. Take Web 2.0 techniques, for example. Google's mapping API does not allow for access to the core data stored on Google's servers—hackers should not be able to upload their own defaced maps. However, the devices that serve maps to the world most definitely have no ability to modify the hub data store to any degree. These servers that provide information to the edge are designed only to send data out, not receive information other than pertinent requests for hub data. In this way, hub-and-edge architecture is maintained to an amazingly usable—and secure—degree.

This architecture is getting so prevalent that some companies have decided to give employees servers outside of the firewall to encourage and enable collaboration while ensuring that hub devices remain secure. While this has often been the norm with web servers, these new servers are now actually providing important data to customers and other external systems in real time. By creating a hub of secure servers that push data out into the ether, the edge systems become useful and secure.

IT for Growth and Development: The Hub-and-Edge Catalyst

The hub and edge in growth and development revolve around economic development with the developed world at the hub and the developing world at the edge. By looking at our previous points, we find that hub-and-edge architecture can improve growth in the developing world by pushing much of the important computing and telecommunications resources into the hands of people who have traditionally been cast out of the international conversation. The goal is to empower the edge of the developing world so that it can grow into a self-sustaining hub that benefits everyone. For the developed world, the challenge is adding new capabilities to the hub.

Take, for example, the rise of mobile phone use in Africa and the Middle East. Through simple SMS networks, craftsmen and farmers can research the going rate for a certain good or type of produce. This levels the playing field between urban and rural areas and is applicable not only in the veldt of Africa but on farms in the heartland of America. By moving data away from hubs—where it is subject to arbitrage charges and other trickery—it has empowered an entire generation to have the same access to information as many large corporations and governments have. While there is still far to go, the hub-and-edge paradigm is bringing many who were once completely disconnected from the world of information into direct contact with the data and news that affect their lives.

Agile Development

One of the most interesting implications of Web 2.0 is the way that it confirms the principles embodied in agile development. Agile development practices are founded on the assumption that there is a huge reward to be gained for being suspicious of the quality of the initial requirements for a system. Agile development methods attempt to frame the creation of any system into a series of small deployable increments that can be put into the hands of users. The experience of deploying and using a system, even one that is small compared to the size of the eventual system, provides the evidence and experience that clear up the true requirements needed to produce the maximum value. The development then proceeds in increments in which a little more of the system is built and deployed to further clarify requirements. As more of the system is built, the increments can contain more functionality and the development can proceed faster.

Agile development is a large umbrella that covers such methods as Extreme Programming, Scrum, the Rational Unified Process, and many others, each of which is aimed at a different problem.

The reigning paradigm in IT has, for years, been the waterfall model. This model assumed a rote set of steps to completing a programming project. Formulated by W. W. Royce in 1970, the Waterfall Model proposed a never-ending process of requirements assessment, programming, testing, and deployment. Each subsequent release required programmers and architects to follow the model over and over again.

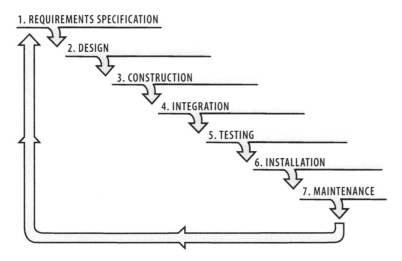

This model presupposed a dedicated team of programmers, testers, and operators that matched the old model of mainframe computing quite well. However, as we have learned, this model is fast becoming, at best, obsolete, and, at worst, wrong.

The Agile Manifesto, published in 2001, assumes that programming teams should focus on one or two requirements, complete them, and then move on to the next set. It includes, but is not limited to:

- Customer satisfaction by rapid, continuous delivery of useful software

- Working software delivered frequently (weeks rather than months)

- Working software as the principal measure of progress

- Even late changes in requirements welcomed

- Close, daily, cooperation between businesspeople and developers

- Face-to-face conversation as the best form of communication

- Projects built around motivated, trusted individuals

- Continuous attention to technical excellence and good design

- Simplicity

- Self-organizing teams
- Regular adaptation to changing circumstances

By looking at computing problems using an agile development viewpoint, we are able to reduce them to a few key aspects and tackle them without bogging down an IT team with minutiae. By creating useful improvements with every iteration of the programming cycle, end-users are better served and administrators are able to add a few basic requirements to their maintenance duties while still watching for errors and problems with the overall system.

The discussion at the forum revealed the use and applicability of agile development principles in several areas. In hub-and-edge discussions, agile development allows programmers and customers to create edge devices that presume specific inputs from the hub and process them in a "closed environment." By "black boxing" many business processes inside an organization, edge devices can accept an input and return a result while ensuring that nothing is broken along the way. By simplifying the programming process, we simplify almost everything in the organization.

But for agile methods to apply, the paradigm must be part of the planning for development and deployment of new systems. This is a tricky business. For example, for a system with 1,000 users, it probably doesn't make sense for all of them to be involved in the iterative development loop. Agile development of large-scale systems may need to involve prototypes or implementations in one smaller part of an organization to allow development to proceed without undue disruption.

Web 2.0: The Perpetual Beta

A corollary truth to agile development is the perpetual beta. Beta software has long been considered untouchable, a sort of untrusted programming stage that allowed architects to inflict their unfinished systems on end-user guinea pigs. Now, however, many major companies call their systems "beta" even if they are being used by millions of people around the world.

Consider, for example, Windows Vista. Microsoft made a number of "release candidate" versions of Vista available to the general public. By offering a free download or disk containing an unfinished copy of Vista, they created good will, gained a wider audience, and caught bugs at the same time.

Another example is Google's Gmail email program. It has been in beta for as long as it has existed, even though millions of people and organizations rely on it on a daily basis.

The perpetual beta is just another name for agile development as applied to an online service. Clearly, however, the perpetual beta is not applicable everywhere. While this is attractive for new services, the approach does have limits. Who would want their bank account to be in perpetual beta? Could we accept beta air traffic control systems?

Mashup Culture in Web 2.0

As we said before, the API platforms built by Web 2.0 leaders have become a catalyst for innovation. Mashups cannot exist without raw materials to combine and recombine, and it is the APIs through which these hub companies drive innovation.

Why are many of these products still in beta stages? Because their creators are faced with the exciting problem of too many users desiring too many things. By creating an open, interconnected platform, they can improve their products incrementally. As user feedback grows, these beta products are able to take on new and exciting aspects. While many companies "sell" their software by saying it does one thing and only one thing, Web 2.0 companies are able to sell combinations of products, promising—and delivering—new ways of thinking about user data, images, and information.

Service-Oriented Architecture

Service-Oriented Architecture (SOA) is a rethinking of computing that emphasizes reusable services as building blocks. The API platforms and mashups of Web 2.0 are an example of SOA but this does not mean that SOA is limited to these examples. The mashups of Web 2.0 are examples of what SOA calls composite applications—applications built out of services.

SOA offers a gateway to reconcile the hub and the edge. The hub can provide certain secure services to the edge that can allow data from the locked down hub into the fuzzy collaborative world of the edge, as appropriate. The hub, like the edge components, knows what to expect and what to distribute. Each of these containers does one or two things extremely well and, because each component is completely closed, fairly securely.

SOA has been widely accepted as an important paradigm in enterprise computing, but implementation has not been fast. One important impact of Web 2.0 could be the acceleration of implementation of SOA in the enterprise, something that could lead to sweeping changes in the industry over time.

The Standards Bottleneck

In each area discussed at the International Research Forum, the call for better standards was repeated over and over again. And despite the strong desire for more and better standards, few expressed hope that the need for standards would be met soon. Standards in security, RWA, and Web 2.0 are given considerable lip service but are rarely implemented in any real way. Clearly, standards are one of the best ways to create and implement reusable computing components. But what is causing the bottleneck?

Web 2.0 is beginning to follow standards for data transmission through syndication and XML as well as common functional systems like user authentication and maintenance. A number of larger companies—Microsoft, Yahoo!, and Google for example—are creating their own standards as they purchase small Web 2.0 companies. This allows for single sign-ins along a number of properties but still creates headaches for programmers wanting to create common standards for international implementation.

Standards for information gathering also affect the implementation of RWA projects. RWA applications create reams and reams of data at an amazing clip. By assessing the system needs at any one time, standards can be created to show and control data feeds in individual cases and for unique groups.

IT security clearly needs standards. A central repository of security best practices and a coordinating group for security certification for practicing IT security professionals would be a godsend.

Finally, in the area of growth and development, the implementation of standards could create easy-to-follow guidelines for information sharing as well as device manufacturing. By setting standards, IT departments could reduce their overall expenditures and avoid wasting energy by implementing a few basic environmental guidelines.

Agile Standards: A New Approach

In many ways the desire for standards represents a sort of greed and impatience that ignores the lessons of agile development. Standards are designed to meet certain needs. The desire for standards is the desire for a working system that everyone can agree on. But experience has shown that standards definition can be both a political battleground and an example of the failure of collaborative design.

Web 2.0's perpetual beta and agile development perhaps show a way out. When a community wants standards for a particular purpose, an experimental period could be declared in which prototype systems are developed and put into limited production. This experience could confirm the requirements that the standards are aimed at meeting and provide insights into how to adjust the standards to make implementation easier. The Internet itself exists today because rather than being created after the development of a standard, as was the case with the then competing Open Systems Interconnect (OSI) protocols, the Internet Engineering Task Force took a pragmatic approach built on rough consensus and running code. We can easily see which of these two approaches succeeded.

Plans for Future Forums

IT is a broad and riveting topic—it is the backbone of today's information economy. By creating a lasting record of its effects on our lives, we create a road map for future study and improvement. Who knows? Perhaps Web 3.0 is right around the corner, fueled by the passion and intellect of hundreds of today's forum participants.

We hope that reading this book has made you interested in being a part of the discussion for future forums. Please visit the International Research Forum web site at *www.international-research-forum.com* to see what others are saying about this book and to examine the agenda for the International Research Forum 2007, which will deal with the overall topic of the transformation of business models.

Appendix: Participants

Participants at the **International Research Forum 2006** come from the highest ranks of the academic, professional, and government communities. This appendix starts with brief biographies of the three authors of this book, Claudia Alsdorf, Lutz Heuser, and Dan Woods. It then provides biographies of the 24 participants who attended the forum so that as you are reading through this book you can find out more about their backgrounds. Finally, it provides biographies that acquaint you with the virtual participants, interviews with whom served to round out and extend the discussions that were started at the forum.

Authors

Claudia Alsdorf has 10 years' experience in the executive management, development, licensing, and commercialization of new consumer electronic products and services across the domains of the Internet, online commerce exchanges, virtual reality, and wireless. For more than five years, she served as Founder and CEO of a global provider of 3D and online exchange products and services called echtzeit AG. In the beginning of 2002 she joined SAP and became Vice President of Communications Development within Global Communications, being responsible for communications strategy and long-term plan development, including the alignment of the communications strategy with noncorporate communication units. In this position she spent one year in the New York office of SAP, working with the Global Marketing team. In 2004 she became the Head of SAP Inspire, the internal venturing group of SAP worldwide. Since 2006 she has also been responsible for SAP Research Communications.

Lutz Heuser, Vice President, SAP Research and Chief Development Architect, SAP AG, is responsible for the overall research portfolio management and the corporate venturing organization. Prof. Heuser's areas of expertise include collaborative business processes, ubiquitous computing and its integration into business applications, blended learning as part of corporate and noncorporate training, as well as security in corporate applications. Prof. Heuser serves on the advisory boards of the imedia Academy, Fraunhofer-Gesellschaft FOKUS, and Fraunhofer-Gesellschaft IPSI. He is a member of the e-Science-Kuratorium, which is monitoring the D-Grid initiative. Prof. Heuser is a Visiting Professor at the National University of Paraguay and an Adjunct Professor of Queensland University of Technology in Brisbane. In 2006 he became a member of the acatech, the Council for Engineering Sciences at the Union of the German Academies of Science and Humanities.

Dan Woods, CTO and Editor of Evolved Media Network, has a background in technology and journalism. Dan has written 10 books about technology-related topics, including *Mashup Corporations,*

Open Source for the Enterprise, and *Enterprise SOA: Designing IT for Business Innovation*. His technology experience began in 1982 with a B.A. in computer science from the University of Michigan. Dan served as CTO of TheStreet.com and CapitalThinking and has been a board member and adviser to many firms. Mid-career, in 1989, Dan earned an M.S. in journalism from the Columbia University Graduate School of Journalism. He then spent six years as a business journalist before returning to technology. At Evolved Media Network, founded in 2002, Dan and his team create books, wikis, white papers, training courses, and documentation to explain the value and workings of technology.

Participants

Witold Abramowicz chairs the Department of Management Information Systems at the Poznan University of Economics, Poland. Prof. Abramowicz's areas of particular interest include information filtering and retrieval to MIS, information in context, and knowledge management in business. He has served an editor or coauthor of 17 books, contributed 35 book chapters, and written over 100 articles published in journals and conference proceedings. He is a member of the editorial board of five international journals. At present, Prof. Abramowicz is working on several projects for the European Union, including enIRaF (enhanced information retrieval and filtering coordinator), SUPER (Semantics Utilized for Process management within and between Enterprises), ASG (Adaptive Services Grid), USE-ME.GOV (USability-drivEn open platform for MobilE GOVernment), and the EastWeb Project.

Nabil R. Adam is a Professor of Computers and Information Systems at Rutgers University in Newark, New Jersey; the Founding Director of the Rutgers University Center for Information Management, Integration, and Connectivity (CIMIC); Director of the Meadowlands Environmental Research Institute; and the Director of the Laboratory for Water Security. Dr. Adam has published numerous technical papers and has coauthored/coedited 10 books, including *Electronic Commerce:*

Technical, Business, and Legal Issues, a book on database issues in GIS, and one on electronic commerce. He is the cofounder and the Executive-Editor-in-Chief of the *International Journal on Digital Libraries* and serves on the editorial board of a number of journals. He is also the cofounder of the IEEE Technical Committee on Digital Libraries.

Fabio Colasanti currently serves as European Commission Director General for Information Society and Media. From 2000 to 2002, he was Director General of EC's Enterprise Directorate General. Prior to that appointment, he was Deputy Head of the Office of EC President Romano Prodi and a Director in the EC's Budget Directorate General, with responsibility for the Resources Directorate. He works regularly in English and French and is also fluent in German and Spanish.

Glenn Edens currently serves as Senior Vice President with Sun Microsystems, Inc., and as Director, Sun Microsystems Laboratories. With an extensive background as a researcher, entrepreneur, corporate strategist, and consultant in telecommunications, entertainment and information technology, Mr. Edens directs Sun's Communications, Media, and Entertainment business as well as research and development at Sun Labs. Mr. Edens cofounded Grid Systems Corporation, the company that developed the first laptop computer. He also founded WaveFrame Corporation, which developed the first all-digital audio workstations for the motion picture, television, and recording industries. WaveFrame received an Oscar from the Academy of Motion Picture Arts and Sciences for its pioneering work in digital audio. Mr. Edens is a member of ACM, IEEE, and the Audio Engineering Society.

José Luis Encarnação was born in Portugal and has been living in the Federal Republic of Germany since 1959. Since 1975, he has been Professor for Computer Science at the Technical University of Darmstadt and is head of the Graphical Interactive Systems Group (GRIS) there. Under Prof. Encarnação's leadership, the INI-GraphicsNet was established. This institutional network is one of the global key players in the area of visualization technologies, new media, and new forms of communications and interaction. He is author or coauthor of more than 500 publications and articles, and is Editor-in-Chief of

Computers & Graphics, published by Elsevier Science. Since July 2001, he has been chairman of the information and communication group of the Fraunhofer Society.

Elgar Fleisch is Professor of Technology Management at the Department of Management, Technology, and Economics at ETH Zürich. He is also Professor for Technology Management and Director of the Institute of Technology Management at the University of St. Gallen, in Switzerland. Prof. Fleisch conducts research on information management issues in the ubiquitously networked world, including the dynamics of information systems in conjunction with business processes and real-world problems. Together with Prof. Friedemann Mattern of the Institute of Pervasive Computing at ETH Zürich, he leads the M-Lab and cochairs the Auto-ID Labs, which specify the infrastructure for the "Internet of Things." Prof. Fleisch is also a cofounder of Intellion AG and Synesix AG and a member of several steering committees in research, education, and industry.

Tai Chuan Foong currently serves as IM Director for Xian Janssen Pharmaceutical Ltd.; as Regional CIO for Janssen-Cilag North Asia; as Chairman of the Johnson & Johnson China IM Council; as a member of the Johnson & Johnson ASPAC IM Council; and as an Advisory Board Member of the Johnson & Johnson SAP Community of Practice. Mr. Foong's areas of professional interest include process excellence, enterprise resource planning systems implementation, strategic enterprise management, change management, IT project management, and Sarbanes-Oxley compliance certification. He is also a Chartered Chemical Engineer in the United Kingdom and a Certified Professional Chemical Engineer in Australia. In addition, Mr. Foong is a member of the CMP Asia Editorial Advisory Board.

Claudia Funke is Partner in the Munich office of McKinsey & Company. She leads the firm's German High Tech Sector, which serves the software and services, datacom, consumer electronics, industrial manufacturing, and aerospace and defense industries. Ms. Funke works primarily for industry leaders in software, IT services, and telecommunication in Europe and North and South America.

Pradeep Khosla is currently Dean of the College of Engineering, Philip and Marsha Dowd Professor of Engineering, and Founding Director of CyLab at Carnegie-Mellon University. Dr. Khosla's research interests are in the areas of reconfigurable and distributed collaborating autonomous systems, agent-based architectures, reconfigurable software, and security for embedded and distributed information systems. He is a Fellow of the IEEE, the American Association of Artificial Intelligence, and the American Association for Advancement of Science. Dr. Khosla's research has resulted in three books and more than 300 articles. He is a consultant to several companies and venture capitalists, and is a cofounder of Quantapoint Inc.

Sanjay Kumar is currently Associate Professor of Operations Management & Information Systems at the XLRI School of Management, Jamshedpur, India. Dr. Kumar conducts executive development programs that attract executives from many South Asian countries besides India, and has also taught in UAE for the XLRI-AIT Institute. He is an SAP-approved faculty member and has conducted faculty-training programs for the SAP University Alliance Program. Dr. Kumar is currently engaged in research in the field of process management, ERP systems implementation and use, and the integration of information in manufacturing and supply chain processes. He is currently collaborating on various research projects with professors at the University of Michigan, Ann Arbor; Merrick School of Business, Baltimore; University of Alabama, Huntsville; and Kelley School of Business, Indiana. In India, he is collaborating with faculty from IIT Kanpur, LIBA Chennai, and IIM Indore.

Peter Kürpick is a Member of the Executive Board of Software AG, having joined the company in April 2005. In his current role, Dr. Kürpick is responsible for the company's cross-vision business unit, which includes research and development, product management, and product marketing. Dr. Kürpick started his career in IT in 1998 as a software developer and served as Senior Vice President, SAP, where he was responsible for major parts of the SAP NetWeaver stack.

Martin Merry manages the Semantic and Adaptive Systems Department at Hewlett-Packard Laboratories in Bristol, England. Subsequent to research works into Mathematical Logic at the universities of Manchester and Cambridge, Mr. Merry joined GEC Research to work on program verification. For the last five years he has managed HP's research investment in the Semantic Web, where he has been heavily involved in defining the Semantic Web standards RDF, OWL, and SPARQL; the development of Jena, HP's Open Source Semantic Web development environment; and the deployment of a number of Semantic Web–based applications within HP and with HP's customers.

Hao Min is currently Research Director of Auto-ID Labs at Fudan University. He started the Auto-ID Center China in 2002 and served as Research Director. Prof. Min's research areas include VLSI architecture, RF and mixed signal IC design, digital signal processing, and image processing. He has published more than 50 papers in journals and conferences.

Deependra Moitra is currently Associate Vice President & General Manager (Research) at Infosys Technologies. A corporate executive and practitioner-scholar, Mr. Moitra works at the intersection of technology, strategy, and innovation. In addition, he specializes in technology and competitive advantage, management of emerging information technologies, globalization of R&D and software development, and strategic innovation management. He currently serves on the editorial boards of more than a dozen leading international journals. Mr. Moitra is a senior member of the IEEE, IEEE Computer Society, and IEEE Engineering Management Society. He is also a member of the Association of Computing Machinery (ACM), the Academy of Management, and the Institute of Management Science (INFORMS). His two books, *R&D Externalization & Competitive Advantage* and *China and India: Opportunities and Threats for the Global Software Industry* (coauthored) will be published in 2007.

Max Mühlhäuser is Professor of Computer Science at the Technical University of Darmstadt. Since 1989, Prof. Mühlhäuser has worked as either professor or visiting professor at universities in Germany, Austria, France, Canada, and the U.S. Prof. Mühlhäuser heads the Telecooperation Division and the Departmental Computing Center within the Informatics Department, the campuswide center of research excellence in e-learning, and further initiatives in Darmstadt. His core research interests include development support for next-generation Internet applications, mainly in the areas of ubiquitous, ambient, and mobile computing and commerce; e-learning; multimodal interaction, distributed multimedia, and continuous media; hypermedia and the Semantic Web; and pervasive security.

Mandi Mzimba is Senior Science and Technology Representative to Europe for South Africa's National Department of Science and Technology. In this role, Dr. Mzimba actively promotes and strengthens research and development in a bilateral cooperation with the European Commission and facilitates investment into scientific infrastructure and major research programs that address South African needs. Dr. Mzimba, as a Deputy Director for the National Department of Health, Pretoria, is responsible for the development of district health systems. She is a founding director of Imvuno Holdings (Pty) Ltd., a women's investment company.

Ike Nassi is the Senior Vice President at SAP Research, Americas, where he and his group explore advanced enterprise technologies and applications for use in the emerging multinational corporate environment. He founded Firetide Inc., a wireless mesh networking company, serving as Executive Vice President, CTO, and member of the Board. He also helped start the Computer History Museum in Mountain View, California, where he currently serves as an active member of the Board of Trustees. Dr. Nassi currently serves on the advisory boards of the Electrical Engineering and Computer Science Department of Northwestern University and the MIS Department of the Eller College of Management at the University of Arizona. He also helped start Encore Computer Corporation, a symmetric multiprocessing pioneer.

Maria E. Orlowska is Professor in Information Systems at the University of Queensland, School of Information Technology and Electrical Engineering in Brisbane, Australia. In addition, she is the Head of Data and Knowledge Engineering Division and a Deputy Head of the ITEE School. Dr. Orlowska is one of founders of the Distributed Systems Technology Centre, DSTC Pty Ltd., and a Distinguished Research Fellow of the DSTC. Currently she is the convener of the Enterprise Information Infrastructure ARC Research Network. She is a member of the editorial boards of eight international journals. Dr. Orlowska's research interests include database systems, data mining, workflow technology, e-business collaboration, business process modeling and verification, high-performance systems, transaction processing, distributed and integrated databases, and information retrieval. Dr. Orlowska's research contributions appear in over 280 published research papers in peer-reviewed international journals and conference proceedings.

Hartmut Raffler is Head of Information and Communications (IC), a division within Siemens Corporate Technology, the research department of Siemens, with subsidiaries in Munich, Princeton, and Beijing. The main topics covered by IC are smart networks, intelligent systems, knowledge management, IT security, and human-computer cooperation. Since 1979, he has been with Siemens AG, Corporate Technology. Mr. Raffler also lectures at the TU Munich and serves on several scientific boards, including the Max-Plank Institute and Fraunhofer Gesellschaft. In addition, he is an editor of *it- Information Technology* magazine, published by Oldenbourg Wissenschaftsverlag GmbH.

Justin Rattner is an Intel Senior Fellow and Director of Intel's Corporate Technology Group. He also serves as the corporation's CTO. He heads Intel's microprocessor, communications, and systems technology labs and Intel Research. He is a longstanding member of Intel's Research Council and Academic Advisory Council. Mr. Rattner currently serves as the Intel executive sponsor for Cornell University, where he serves on the External Advisory Board for the School of Engineering.

Alexander Schill is Professor of Computer Networks at Dresden University of Technology. His major research interests are distributed systems and middleware, high-performance communication and multimedia, and advanced teleservices such as teleteaching and tele-working. Prof. Schill is the author and coauthor of a large number of publications on computer networking, including several books.

David Schrader is the lead strategist and a marketing director for the Teradata Solutions marketing group. Dr. Schrader works with Teradata's various industry organizations in the retail, financial, insurance, travel, transportation, government, and manufacturing sectors to leverage decision analytics in industry portfolios. He is currently leading the marketing activities for the Teradata Application Platform. He is also a popular speaker at Teradata's User Groups in North America, and at international Teradata Universe Events in Paris, Seoul, Tokyo, and Sydney. Dr. Schrader sits on the Board for the Integrated Media Systems Center at the University of Southern California and is also on its Scientific Advisory Board. He is a trustee of the Marketing Sciences Institute and is on the Research Committee for the Teradata Center at the Duke University School of Business.

Michael Schrage is a researcher at the MIT Media Lab and senior adviser to MIT's Security Studies Program, as well as a lecturer at Sloan School of Management's executive education programs on new product management. He is also a visiting professor at KTH, Sweden's Royal Institute of Technology, and advises organizations on the economics of innovation through rapid experimentation, simulation, and digital design. Michael Schrage performs nonclassified work for the National Security Council, DARPA, and the Pentagon's Office of Net Assessment. As a columnist for *CIO* magazine, he has also written about innovation issues for the *Harvard Business Review, Sloan Management Review, Fortune,* the *Financial Times,* the *Washington Post, Strategy+Business,* and the *Wall Street Journal.*

Wolfgang Wahlster is the Director and CEO of DFKI, the German Research Center for Artificial Intelligence, and a Professor of Computer Science at Saarland University. Prof. Wahlster has published more than 170 technical papers and seven books on language technology and intelligent user interfaces. He serves on a number of international advisory boards and is a member of the supervisory boards of various IT and venture capital firms. Prof. Wahlster is an AAAI Fellow, an ECCAI Fellow, and a GI Fellow. He was the first German computer scientist to be elected as a foreign member of the Royal Swedish Nobel Prize Academy of Sciences. In 2004, he was elected full member of the German Academy of Natural Scientists Leopoldina, founded in 1652, and of acatech, the Council for Engineering Sciences at the Union of the German Academies of Science and Humanities.

Virtual Participants

Bill "Ches" Cheswick was Chief Scientist for Lumeta. Ches worked for nearly 30 years on operating-systems security, including 13 years of service at AT&T/Lucent/Bell Labs where he began the Internet Mapping Project. The technology used for this project became the genesis of Lumeta. An internationally acclaimed expert on security, Ches cowrote the bible for firewall management, *Firewalls and Internet Security: Repelling the Wily Hacker*, first published by Addison Wesley in 1994. His depth of knowledge has resulted in his being a frequent consultant to government agencies and an advisor to law enforcement for high-profile computer crimes. Ches left Lumeta in September 2006 and is currently a free agent.

Lee Felsenstein, a hardware engineer, is best known for his long-standing efforts to demystify technology and give more people in the U.S. and abroad access to the benefits of ICT. In the 1970s, he helped run the Community Memory Project, a public-access electronic bulletin board in Berkeley, California. Later, he designed the Osborne 1 computer, the first "luggable" computer. Today, he heads the Fonly Institute, a consulting R&D organization in Palo Alto, California, that creates "sustainable systems that facilitate economic self-development in rural and underserved communities." Fonly—the name derives from "if only"—has received much attention for a bicycle-powered ICT system it designed for refugee villages in remote areas of Laos.

Mark Kobayashi-Hillary is a London-based British writer and researcher. Mr. Kobayashi-Hillary is the author of *Outsourcing to India: The Offshore Advantage* and *Building a Future with BRICs: The Next Decade for Offshoring,* coauthor of *Global Services: Moving to a Level Playing Field,* and was a contributor to the book *Technology and Offshore Outsourcing Strategies.* He is a director of the UK National Outsourcing Association and a founding member of the British Computer Society working party on offshoring.

John Musser is the founder of ProgrammableWeb.com, the online resource covering mashups, APIs, and other topics relating to the Web-as-platform. He is a Seattle-based technology consultant, writer, and teacher. During his 20-year career in software development, Mr. Musser has shipped five award-winning software products in three industries working with companies including Electronic Arts, Credit Suisse, MTV, and Bell Labs. He has taught at Columbia University and the University of Washington and has written for a variety of technology publications on the topic of software development.

Nandan M. Nilekani is cofounder and CEO of Infosys, one of India's largest software companies, with more than 66,000 employees and a market capitalization of more than $30 billion. Mr. Nilekani is one of the most ardent and eloquent advocates for India's software industry, and he has spoken on the subject at the World Economic Forum in Davos, Switzerland, at the Clinton Global Initiative in New York, and on many other occasions. He is also the man who informed Thomas Friedman, author of *The Flat World,* that "the playing field is being leveled."

Tim O'Reilly is the founder and CEO of O'Reilly Media, a publisher of technical books and journals headquartered in Sebastopol, California. The company also publishes online through the O'Reilly Network and hosts conferences on technology topics. Among these is the Web 2.0 conference, jointly produced with CMP Media. He is an activist for open source, open standards, and sensible intellectual property laws. Since 1978, Mr. O'Reilly has led the company's pursuit of its core goal: to be a catalyst for technology change by capturing and transmitting the knowledge of "alpha geeks" and other innovators. His active engagement with technology communities drives both the company's product development and its marketing. Mr. O'Reilly describes his company as one where advocacy, meme-making, and evangelism are key tenets of the business philosophy.

Tim Wood, Technical Project Manager of the Grameen Foundation, specializes in applying information technology to address the problems of poverty and health in developing countries. After 12 years at Microsoft working on software development, Tim spent two years working with the Bill & Melinda Gates Foundation where he defined the Information Technology Strategy for their Global Health Program and reviewed grant proposals. He joined the Grameen Technology Center in 2002 to focus on replicating the Grameen Village Phone program. Tim brings a broad range of technical and business expertise and a valued perspective on technology initiatives for developing countries.

Greg Wyler is the founder of Terracom, Rwanda's largest telecommunications company. A Boston native, Wyler founded Terracom in 2003 as a competitor to that nation's state-run monopoly, RwandaTel. With the help of investors, Wyler purchased RwandaTel two years later, and today is the country's only fixed-line operator and its largest cellular carrier. In less than three years, Terracom has succeeded in installing fiber-optic cables connecting Rwanda's largest cities, Kigali and Butare, and has established nationwide wireless broadband with the help of solar-powered cellular towers and 3G broadband.

www.ingramcontent.com/pod-product-compliance
Lightning Source LLC
Chambersburg PA
CBHW051238050326
40689CB00007B/979